D0192212

EQUIPMENT TECHNIQUES

REORDER # 2501EQ

CONTENTS

ACKNOWLEDGMENTS

Editor in Chief	**Laurie Clark Humpal**
Art Director	**David M. Pratt**
Photographers	**Blake Miller** **Greg Ochocki** (Front Cover) **Charlie Arneson** (Back Cover)
Contributing Editors	**Bob Clark** **Gary Clark** **Ed Christini** **Doug Kelly** **Dennis Pulley**
Technical Editors	**Jim Dexter** SCUBAPRO **Don Frueh** SCUBAPRO **Alan Edmunnd** HENDERSON AQUATICS **Steve Lamphear** U.S. DIVERS **Paul Leszczynski** U.S. DIVERS **Chris Kralj** **Karen Rapier** **Bob Schaible**
Proofing Editor	**Linda J. Clark**
Graphic Designer	**Laurinda M. Baker**

Special Thanks To:

Paul Caputo ◆ **Dr. Andrew M. Norris, M.D.**
Brent Goetzel, Pulagic Pressure Systems

FOREWORD

WHY SPECIALTY TRAINING? The answer to "why specialty training?" is quite simple. An entry level course provides you with the motor skills, equipment knowledge, and minimum open water experience needed to be considered a safe diver. However, an Open Water Diver Course does not a specialist make.

Specialty training has two primary objectives: to prepare you for new diving situations, and to improve your level of skill. The SSI Specialty Diver Program provides an excellent introduction to a variety of different diving subjects such as Deep Diving, Boat Diving, Night Diving/Limited Visibility, and many others. These courses are designed to enhance both the enjoyment and safety of each new situation. Specialty training also develops your current level of skill to a much higher level. For example, you may have learned how to follow a compass in your entry level course—SSI's Navigation Specialty course can teach you how to navigate! A specialty course takes you clearly beyond what you may have learned in your Open Water Diver Course.

Each specialty generates its own excitement and opens its own doors. Not every specialty is appropriate to every diver or diving level. Some specialties may not be available in your area, but can be enjoyed when traveling. Every specialty, however, can open new vistas for the diver who wishes to explore all the adventures scuba diving can provide!

The SSI Specialty Diver Program offers the opportunity, through continuing education, to accelerate the learning process that otherwise could only be gained through significant, time-consuming experience. You can quickly prepare yourself to be comfortable in whatever diving situations apply to you personally. Here is a simple, inexpensive way to gain knowledge, experience, safety and recognition, in classes tailored to your specific interests!

THE SSI SPECIALTY DIVER PROGRAM OFFERS THE OPPORTUNITY TO ACCELERATE THE LEARNING PROCESS THAT COULD OTHERWISE BE GAINED ONLY THROUGH TIME-CONSUMING EXPERIENCE.

BASIC DIVING EQUIPMENT

1

CHAPTER 1:
BASIC DIVING EQUIPMENT

Snorkeling equipment is characterized by its simplicity of design and ease of use. The lack of moving mechanical parts makes this type of equipment easy to maintain, easy to use, and very reliable. It also tends to be the most personal equipment, which means fit is one of the most important aspects.

In this chapter, we will cover the mask, snorkel and fins, exposure suits, and weight systems commonly used for snorkeling and scuba diving. Let's begin by taking a look at why today's divers need a broad-based knowledge of equipment, and how this manual is structured to meet our knowledge objectives.

INTRODUCTION

When scuba diving was young, the few hardy individuals pursuing the sport knew their equipment inside and out. When equipment failed or didn't fit just right, these divers made repairs and adaptations themselves—often right in the field. Dive stores and trained technicians were scarce in those days. Thus, scuba's pioneers were each often a mixture of engineer, inventor, craftsman, and daredevil

Today's divers, however, represent diverse levels of interest and experience. Indeed, there are still many divers whose devotion to scuba is as intense as that of the pioneer divers, but the majority of today's divers view the sport as a leisurely activity. Their attitude towards equipment is that of the discerning consumer. They want reliable, comfortable equipment that meets their individual needs and skill levels.

What You Will Learn

There are many resources for the sport diver regarding equipment. Dive stores, manufacturers and diving publications offer a wealth of information. The SSI *Open Water Diver* manual provides excellent explanations of equipment features, fit, and function. Although there is some review, the information covered in the *Open Water Diver* manual is not duplicated in this book. The focus of this manual is to enhance the diver's ability to be better informed when selecting, maintaining, repairing, and packing his or her diving equipment.

Each section in this manual includes a brief explanation of the purpose and function of that piece of equipment. Areas covered in the *Equipment Techniques* manual include:

- **Selection:** Details on the variety of styles, designs and constructions of dive equipment which are considered when making a purchasing decision.

- **Adjustment:** How to customize and improve your equipment, and how to make minor alterations when needed.

- **Care and Maintenance:** Advanced techniques, including the lubrication, cleaning, and parts replacement (and when to leave it to a qualified service technician).

- **Field Repairs:** How to make minor repairs and adjustments when equipment breaks down at the site.

- **Transportation:** Methods for protecting your equipment while traveling either locally or long distance.

- **Storage:** Methods for insuring the reliability and longevity of your equipment while storing it.

The SSI *Equipment Techniques* Specialty course will not make you an equipment technician. Rather, the information presented will help you make better choices regarding equipment. With rapid advances in diving technology, divers need to constantly update their equipment knowledge.

Purchasing Equipment

Divers who are serious will learn quickly that purchasing their own equipment and knowing how to care for it will vastly enhance the diving experience.

When deciding to purchase equipment you should visit your local SSI dive store for direction on selecting the best equipment for your needs. Function, durability, fit and comfort are all major concerns. When you are buying equipment that you are unfamiliar with, or a device with a specialized use, you should have proper training in how to use it before diving in the open water.

Diving equipment is manufactured under stringent specifications today. By completing your warranty card and returning it to the manufacturer, they will be able to contact you directly for any reason, such as equipment updates (Figure 1-1). Usually, the store where you purchased your equipment will also have a record on file, so they can also contact you. If you are not one who usu-ally fills out warranty cards, ask the dive store to help you do so. Most service oriented stores will gladly help.

Remember, how-ever, that any time there appears to be a problem with a piece of your diving equip-ment, it should be

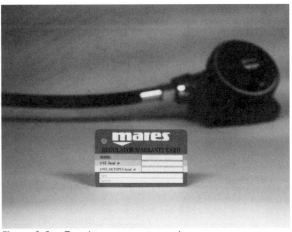

Figure 1-1 *Regulator warranty card.*

repaired by a qualified service technician at a dive store before it is used. Only by having your equipment serviced annually, can you keep your warranty in force.

Now that we have looked at the many reasons why equipment know-how is so important, let's begin by looking first at the most basic equipment—the mask, fins, and snorkel. Despite the lack of moving parts, the maintenance of these basic items is just as important as that of the more complex diving equipment.

MASKS

To see under water, the diver's eyes must be surrounded with air. When immersed in water, the human eye loses its focusing power because of the different speeds at which light travels when in air and water, and the way the eye interprets light. Light passes through air faster than it does through water because water is denser than air. This causes light to "bend," which is called refraction.

The surface of the eye, the cornea, is composed mostly of water. Thus the eye normally interprets the refraction of light from air to the water of the cornea. If the eye is immersed in water, however, the light is refracted in the surrounding water as well as the water of the cornea. The result is that vision becomes blurred. When a diving mask surrounds the eye with air, the eye is returned to its natural environment, and vision becomes possible under water.

Selection

There is a large variety of styles of masks. The two basic types, however, are the *low volume* and *high volume* masks.

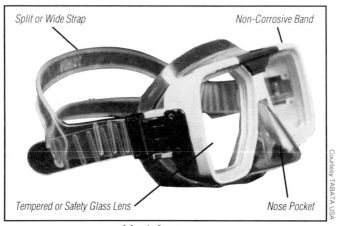

Split or Wide Strap

Non-Corrosive Band

Tempered or Safety Glass Lens

Nose Pocket

Courtesy TABATA USA

Mask features.

■ **Low vs. High Volume:** The low volume has less air space and a pocket for the nose. These masks usually fit people with smaller or more slender faces better than high volume styles. A silicone mask skirt allows light to penetrate even the lowest volume mask, overcoming the feeling of "tunnel vision" created by black rubber.

High volume masks usually feature side panels which increase the field of vision. These masks have a larger internal volume, and sometimes include a purge valve for clearing water.

■ **Purge Valves:** Purge valves were very popular in the 1970's, but their use has decreased over the years. Older purge valves were made of black rubber that would crack easily and lead to a leaky mask. With the invention of the popular low volume masks there became less need for a purge. The use of silicone has improved purge valve systems and they are again gaining in popularity.

■ **Silicone vs. Rubber:** Black rubber mask skirts and straps have been upstaged by clear and colored silicone. The softer silicone can almost mold to your face, preventing small leaks, plus it is durable because the silicone is almost resistant to oxidation and deterioration from the ozone. The life of a silicone product is sometimes three to four times that of a black rubber product. Although silicone masks will cost more, the above benefits still make them the most popular on the market.

■ **Corrective Lenses:** Depending on what type of vision problem you have, you may need to purchase a mask with corrective lenses. Many people who are mildly myopic (nearsighted) may need no correction at all because the magnifying property of the water can actually correct their vision. Should you need vision correction, however, there are three options available: 1) Purchase a mask with lenses that are pre-ground to an approximate prescription, 2) Have an optician bond prescription lenses to the inside of the mask, or 3) Wear contact lenses.

The nearsighted diver may choose to correct vision with optical lenses measured in *diopters*—corrective lenses offered by manufacturers to replace stock lenses in their particular mask (Figure 1-2). There are also many opticians who specialize in making prescription masks. Your

Figure 1-2 *Corrective lenses.*

local SSI store can arrange for this service or refer a qualified optician. Should you choose to wear contact lenses while diving, be aware that the lenses must be gas permeable so that changes in pressure will not cause bubbles to form between the contact lens and your eye.

Adjustment

Even a good-fitting mask can be uncomfortable if the strap is too tight. The strap should be tight enough to maintain the seal, but not so tight that it causes a squeeze. If your mask will not seal without being tight, recheck the fit. Over time the mask skirt may stretch, or your face shape may change due to weight loss or gain. You might need to try other masks in an attempt to find one that fits better.

For added comfort, you may want to replace your mask strap with a neoprene replacement strap. They are easily adjusted, stay in place, and do not tangle hair as much as rubber or silicone straps (Figure 1-3).

Figure 1-3 *Neoprene mask strap.*

Care and Maintenance

Prior to each dive, use a commercial defogger to prevent fogging. Be sure to follow the the directions for use on the container. Wash your mask after each use to keep it in top shape.

- **Strap:** Check for cracks and wear, especially where the strap fits into the locking device.

- **Mask Skirt:** If a mask that once fit you well now leaks, check to see if the skirt has a small hole or tear in it. If damaged, the mask skirt will need to be replaced by a professional scuba retailer.

- **Lens:** A broken lens should be replaced by a repair technician. Your SSI dive store would be glad to help.

Field Repairs

There may be times when you are at a dive site and you develop a mask problem. The best defense is to always carry a back-up mask, however, you may be able to perform minor field repairs so you can continue your dive. Any major problems will need to be handled by a qualified technician, or the mask may need to be sent back to the manufacturer.

- **Purge Leaks:** If your mask is leaking you may have a problem in your purge valve. If your mask is a newer model, check to make sure that the purge valve is in place and that there is no foreign matter in it. If it appears ok, the leak is probably the result of damage to the "spider," or the part of the mask that holds the purge valve in place. Your local retailer will be able to replace this part for you.

■ **Broken Strap:** If your mask strap breaks, you should replace it with a spare from your Spare Parts and Repair kit. Should you need to borrow a strap that doesn't quite fit, the strap can be narrowed by trimming it with scissors. Trim it a little at a time to make sure you don't cut too much away (Figure 1-4). If your mask requires a special strap, you may want to purchase extras when you buy your mask.

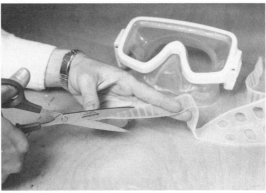

Figure 1-4 *Trimming a mask strap to size.*

Storage

Some new masks come with a protective plastic box. These boxes, or the more expensive crush-proof dry boxes, are your best insurance against broken lenses and cracked seals that sometimes occur when traveling (Figure 1-5).

You should only store your mask after it is completely dry, and it should be stored in a cool, dry place. You may want to remove the mask strap for storage to prevent pressure spots which may cause addi-tional wear.

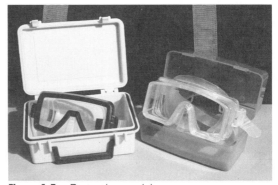

Figure 1-5 *Protective mask boxes.*

Preparing New Masks

Before using brand new equipment that is right out of the box you will probably need to do some minor preparation. Some silicone masks that are purchased may have a residual film on the lens that is left over from manufacturing. This film will need to be removed before your new mask is used or you will have problems with your lens fogging.

Scrub the lens of new masks with a mild cleaner such as toothpaste or Johnson's Baby Shampoo. Mask cleaners are also available at your local dive store. After scrubbing the mask, make sure you thoroughly wash it in warm, fresh water to remove any cleaning residue.

> **Warning:** Do not clean your mask lens with any cleanser that could be harmful to your eyes. Read the label of any cleanser before using it on your mask.

FINS

Today, fins come in a wide variety of shapes, designs and colors, and are constructed of many different materials—rubber, injection molded thermoplastics such as polyethelene, polyurethane, and other elastomeric thermoplastics, or a combination of the above to create a multi-compound fin. The combination of elastomeric thermoplastics and rigid thermoplastics creates a fin that is flexible, yet powerful.

Selection

The two basic styles of fins are the full-foot fin and the open-heel fin. However, there are various designs, colors and levels of durability to choose from within these two styles.

■ **Blade Design:** The most noticeable difference between fins is blade design. Some blades are vented while others have ribs or channels. All of these blades are designed to cut down water resistance while increasing the power, so each kick propels you farther with less effort (Figure 1-6a & b).

■ **Durability:** Another important aspect of fin selection is durability. Most fins will maintain their stiffness and ability to function, but not all of them will still look good after their first dive trip. To select a thermoplastic fin that will be durable, look for one that is made of an abrasion resistant, yet elastic material. This combination will provide a fin that has a tough enough surface to avoid abrasion, without having a blade that is too stiff to be comfortable. Of course, black rubber is also very resistant to abrasion and temperature.

Other features to think about when selecting a fin are the buoyancy of the fin (whether it sinks or floats), the visibility of the fin (will it be easily

Courtesy SCUBAPRO

Figure 1-6a *Vented fin blade design.*

Courtesy U.S. DIVERS

Figure 1-6b *Non-vented fin blade design.*

seen in poor visibility), and the use of the fin (will it be used in the same or differing environmental conditions). All of these factors determine whether you will be able to find one fin to suit all of your needs. For example, a fin that you wear with your dry suit in cold water might not be appropriate for warm, tropical water when you are wearing only a dive skin.

One last, but very important aspect of selection is comfort. Your fins must fit you, and fit your leg strength. A fin that is too stiff or has a very large blade may cause fatigue or leg cramping.

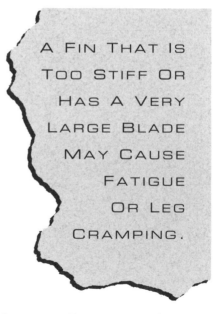

A FIN THAT IS TOO STIFF OR HAS A VERY LARGE BLADE MAY CAUSE FATIGUE OR LEG CRAMPING.

Adjustment

Once you have selected a pair of fins you will want to try them out; your local retailer may have a pool you can use. You may want to return them if they are uncomfortable, or you may want to make a few adjustments before trying them in the open water.

■ **Straps:** When you adjust your fins make sure you are wearing the proper booties for the environment you will be diving in, and then tighten the strap so it is snug, but not too tight. You may want to shorten your fin straps if they are exceptionally long to keep them out of the way.

Care and Maintenance

Soak your fins in fresh water after every dive, making sure to get all of the sand rinsed out of the buckles. Excess debris may cause the buckles to become stuck and difficult to use. Allow your fins to dry thoroughly out of direct sunlight. Do not leave the fins in the trunk of your car on a hot day, for heat can distort the shape of thermoplastic fins.

When checking fins for wear and damage, the rule is, "worn fin straps and buckles can be replaced, worn fin pockets mean new fins." There is no way to fix a hole, tear, or crack in the fin pocket. You will want to carry extra straps and buckles with you in your spare parts kit. Be sure and obtain directions from your local retailer on how to replace a buckle.

To lengthen the life of rubber fins and to make them look nicer, occasionally spray them with a light coating of silicone, but *avoid* the straps and buckles. Do not use any petroleum based products or silicone sprays that contain hydrocarbon propellants. These products will have a detrimental effect on rubber and some thermoplastic fins. Instead, use a silicone pump spray that is water based (Figure 1-7).

Figure 1-7   *Use a silicone pump spray that is water based and contains no hydrocarbon propellants.*

Field Repairs

About the only field repairs you will be able to make on fins will be to replace your straps or buckles should they break. As with masks straps, if you do not have the correct fin strap you may be able to make it fit by cutting it down.

Storage

When transporting or storing fins, make sure they are stored flat. The blade or pocket may curl if a heavy object is stored on top of it for a long time, especially in hot temperatures. For this reason, make sure you store your fins in a cool place. Fin pocket inserts will maintain the shape of the foot pockets so they don't get crushed or bent. Make sure they are in place for storage (Figure 1-8). If you don't have any inserts for your fins, you may want to look into purchasing some.

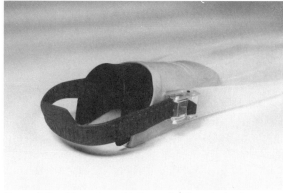

Figure 1-8 *Store fins with fin pocket inserts in place.*

SNORKELS

At first glance, snorkels appear to be the most simplistic diving equipment—nothing more than a breathing tube. However, many features have been added to make the snorkel much easier to clear and more comfortable to use. By adding purge valves and allowing for drainage out the bottom, manufacturers have made snorkel clearing nearly fool-proof.

Snorkels have been improved by making mouthpieces from silicone. And by shaping snorkels to fit the head and mouth better, and by adding features that allow mouthpieces to rotate, manufacturers have made snorkels more comfortable.

Selection

You will want to select a snorkel that is comfortable, but it must also fit your diving needs. If you plan on doing a lot of snorkeling or surface swimming, you will know what type of snorkel you like to use. However, if you rarely use your snorkel it is more important that you buy a high-quality one. Divers who snorkel infrequently require a snorkel that breathes and clears easily because they won't be as comfortable should they need to use it in an emergency.

Most snorkels are made of either black rubber, silicone, plastic, or some combination of the above. Most snorkels now come with a purge valve to keep it dryer. Some snorkels even come with a one-way valve in the bore to stop any water from entering the snorkel on the surface (Figure 1-9). Another snorkel now has a two-purge system to allow for faster draining and a dryer airway. When it comes to bore design you will have a choice of the J-shape or a corrugated snorkel.

As you can see, the snorkel may appear to be a simple piece of equipment, but a lot of engineering has gone into making it the comfortable, easy-clearing device it is today.

Care and Maintenance

Occasionally check the snorkel for wear. Inspect the mouthpiece for tears and check that the bite block is not damaged or bitten off. If it is, you may need to replace it. Make sure the snorkel keeper is not damaged, and that there are no cracks in the the snorkel bore.

If your snorkel has a purge valve, you will want to check the seal periodically for cracks. Check the seal by sealing the top of the bore with your hand, and then gently inhaling (Figure 1-10). If you cannot inhale then the purge is functioning properly, if you can inhale, then there is a leak in the valve and it will need to be replaced. If your snorkel has a valve in the bore (See Figure 1-9) the snorkel will always leak during this test.

You may want to use some brightly colored or flourescent tape to add a bright band at the top of the snorkel. This bright band will allow boaters and other people to see you on the surface.

Last, be sure and soak your snorkel in fresh water after every dive to keep it clean and improve its life.

Field Repairs

The only field repairs you will probably need to make on your snorkel will be to replace a lost or torn keeper, mouthpiece, or purge valve. Because there are various sizes and styles of snorkel keepers and purge valves, it is always best to be prepared with extras in your spare parts kit.

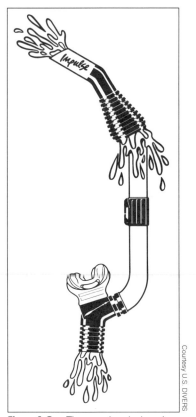

Courtesy U.S. DIVERS

Figure1-9 *The annular drain valve allows the snorkel to stay dry on the surface.*

Figure1-10 *Checking the purge valve.*

Storage

A snorkel is easy to store and transport; the only thing to remember is to remove it from your mask and to make sure it is stored flat. The tube may compress if a heavy object is stored on top of it for a long time, especially in hot temperatures.

EXPOSURE SUITS

Water absorbs body heat twenty-five times faster than air. Even warm water will "pull" heat from the body. Ideally, the normal body temperature of 98.6°F (37° C) should be maintained.

The three basic types of exposure suits that we will discuss include lycra® suits, wet suits, and dry suits. There are general guidelines about the type of exposure suit you're likely to need based on temperature ranges. However, the amount of protection used depends ultimately on the particular needs of the diver.

LYCRA® SUITS

At temperatures above 91° F (33° C) many divers will stay comfortable without protective wear, but it is a good idea to at least be protected from sunburn, the marine environment and equipment that might cause chafing. Lightweight lycra® dive suits provide protection for temperatures above 80° F (27° C), and in fact, one manufacturer of lycra® suits claims that a lycra® "skin" is 45% warmer than wearing nothing at all (Figure 1-11).

As lycra® suits have become more popular, new materials have been created to increase the warmth and protection of these suits, while still maintaining their comfort and flexibility. Darlexx® is a fabric made by bonding 3 layers of material together. A thin membrane of thermoplastic film is sandwiched between two layers of lycra® to create a fabric that is waterproof, windproof and breathable, yet is

Figure 1-11 *Lightweight lycra® dive suits.*

still neutrally buoyant. Polartec® is a fabric with a lycra® shell, a windproof polyurethane barrier, and a velour interior. This unique fabric is soft, warm, dries fast, and wicks away moisture from your body. Durasoft Lite® is a fabric that provides twice the warmth of Darlexx®, yet is still neutrally buoyant. Like Polartec®, it also has a plush liner that is breathable. Darlexx® suits have also been improved by adding 2mm neoprene panels at certain points to improve flexibility.

All lycra® skins can be worn by themselves, layered together for increased thermal protection, or worn under wet suits to aid in getting the wet suit on and off.

Layering a lycra® suit under a wet suit.

Care and Maintenance

Lycra® suits should be washed in fresh water after every dive, and should be laundered occasionally. Most lycra® suits can be washed in the washing machine and hung to dry. Follow the care label on your suit for specific laundering instructions. Lycra® suits can be snagged and damaged by the Velcro® straps on your BC, or by rough textures such as concrete or wood. Be careful when putting on and taking off our BC. Because the seams of most lycra® suits are exposed, you will be able to mend any rips in the seams that might occur.

Storage

Store your lycra suit in a dry, cool place after it has been cleaned and thoroughly dried. Hang your suit on a wide, plastic hanger in a closet to help keep its shape.

WET SUITS

As you already learned in your Open Water Diver class, wet suits keep you warm by creating an insulative layer of warm water around your body. Wet suits are by far the most common form of thermal protection for divers and they come in a variety of thicknesses, styles and colors depending on your taste and diving environment. Wet suits are made of foam neoprene that is produced in one of two ways.

Wet suits are the most common form of thermal protection.

- ■ **Chemically Blown:** Chemically blown neoprene is used in 99% of todays wet suits. It is made by mixing the rubber ingrediants with a a blowing agent. During the curing process the foaming agent vaporizaed to create gas bubbles that form the cellular structure of the neoprene.

- ■ **Nitrogen Blown:** Nitrogen blown neoprene is the original process for making neoprene and entails pressurizing uncured rubber in a chamber at extreme pressures and elevated temperatures. When the pressure is released, the nitrogen creates bubbles in the rubber. This process is expensive, but create a high quality neoprene.

Selection

It is important to select a suit that is comfortable and fits your diving needs. How comfortable a suit will be is based on how elastic the neoprene is, and how the exterior fabric is bonded to the rubber. During the manufacturing phase, softeners are mixed in with the rubber to create different grades of neoprene. The softer the neoprene, the more elastic it will be. If too much glue is used when bonding the exterior fabric to the neoprene, it may prohibit how stretchy the fabric is and lessen comfort.

Your susceptibility to cold and your level of activity in the water will dictate how warm your suit should be. Neoprene comes in various sizes from 1 to 7 mm; the thickness of the materials determines how warm the suit will be. The *Guide to Thermal Protection* will help advise you on the thickness needed for various water temperatures (Figure 1-12).

Neoprene that is manufactured for diving is more resistant to pressure than the super light weight "above water" neoprenes that are used for surfing suits. Be aware that these suits will not continue to provide the same warmth under pressure as well as suits that are made for diving.

WET SUIT THICKNESS	WATER TEMPERATURE
⅜ inch or dry suit	35°-50°F (1°-10°C)
⅜ or ¼ Inch	50°-60°F (10°-16°C)
¼ or ³⁄₁₆ inch	60°-70°F (16°-21°C)
³⁄₁₆ or partial ¼ inch	70°-75°F (21°-24°C)
⅛ or partial ³⁄₁₆ inch	75°F (24°C) & above
Lycra® Dive Suit	80°F (27°C) & above

Figure 1-12 *Guide to proper thermal protection.*

■ **Suit Fabrics:** While most early suits used to be unlined, or lined with nylon, there are now other options to choose from such as plush or lycra linings. While nylon is durable and widely used, plush and lycra linings offer increased comfort and flexibility. The one drawback to plush fabrics is that they allow increased water into the suit initially, however, the plush fiber also helps retard water circulation to keep the diver warm. Nylon and lycra are also the most common exterior fabric. Both offer increased durability and aesthetics through the wide variety of color combinations that are available. While lycra provides increased durability and an aesthetic finish to a suit, it is also more expensive. Nylon is the most common fabric used.

■ **Seams:** The type of seams inside your suit will also affect its comfort. Look for seams that are sewn or taped flat, not ridged. The suit will fit better and bend with your body more, plus it will prevent the uncomfortable creases that ridged seams leave in your skin.

■ **Styles:** Once you have decided upon your suit thickness, comfort, fit and color, you will need to choose the style of suit that fits your needs. The basic styles are the one-piece jumpsuit, and the two-piece combination which consists of a farmer john and shorty. You can also create other combinations by layering pieces. For example, you can wear the shorty or farmer john alone in warmer water, while you may want to wear a shorty under your jumpsuit in cooler water.

■ **Custom Fit:** Because divers today come in all shapes and sizes, it can be difficult to find a stock suit to fit. A custom suit is designed to fit your body and cut down on sags and gaps, ensuring less water exchange and therefore less heat loss and greater comfort. The thicker your suit, the more important it is for it to fit right. A heavy, 6 or 7 mm neoprene can be quite uncomfortable if it bulges in the wrong spot.

Adjustment

Should you ever lose weight or change body shape, you can have your suit cut down, or increased so it fits properly. It is easier to cut a suit down, but either process is possible if the changes are kept to 1 or 2 inches. Any larger changes will begin to change the shape of the suit.

Before buying a suit, you may want to check with the retailer to make sure the manufacturer provides a re-cutting service.

There are a variety of accessories that can be added to your suit for convenience and comfort. Pockets can be added to hold knives or lights, while elbow or knee pads increase the life of the suit. A spine pad will provide protection between the diver's back and the tank, as well as lessen the exchange of water inside the suit. Zippers at the wrists and ankles make dressing easier, however they allow more water seepage. Today's more flexible neoprene suits are easier to get into and have helped eliminate the need for extra zippers.

Care and Maintenance

Soak your wet suit in fresh water after every dive and allow it to dry out of direct sunlight. Sunlight will fade the fabric, delaminate the nylon from the rubber, and will cause the neoprene to shrink over time. After multiple uses, wet suits can become soiled with body oils and should be cleaned with a mild detergent (see manufacturer's directions).

Should you tear your suit, you can mend it with wet suit cement. The correct way to apply wet suit cement to a seam or patch is to spread a light coat to both surfaces, then after it dries, reapply a second coat. Once the cement is no longer sticky, lightly press the pieces together and then apply pressure until a proper seal is formed. The repair should sit for 24 hours for maximum strength. Make sure the neoprene is completely dry before attempting any repairs. There are also commercial patch kits available to cover rips, tears, or worn fabric around the knees or elbows. These patches are easily applied with a household iron (Figure 1-13).

Occasionally check velcro straps and twistlocks on the beavertail to see if they need replacement.

Figure1-13 *Commercial patch kits are available for mending wet suits.*

Field Repairs

The most common field problems will be stuck zippers ,and rips or tears to the wet suit fabric. If your zipper sticks, wash it thoroughly with water and then apply a zipper lubricant. To repair tears, follow the procedure listed under maintenance. Make sure the suit is completely dry before applying cement. A repair that dries for 1-2 hours may provide reasonable strength for emergency use in the field.

Transportation

When you are transporting your wet suit, fold it neatly inside your suitcase or dive bag. Avoid stuffing it in the bag or packing it under heavy items which can damage the zipper or crease the neoprene.

Storage

Store your wet suits by hanging them on a wide plastic or wood hanger. Over time, folded wet suits will form a permanent crease in the neoprene. Store your suit in a dry, cool closet, and you may want to encase it in a plastic bag for extra protection from damage by the ozone or insects

Gloves, boots and other neoprene products should be cared for and stored in the same manner as your wet suit.

DRY SUITS

Unlike wet suits, dry suits have little or no inherent insulating capabilities. The suit itself is designed to keep you dry, not warm, so the warmth must come from what you wear underneath. For very cold water or extended exposure, you can wear special dry suit "underwear," while warmer water temperatures might only require cotton workout clothes.

Although dry suits are not extremely complicated, they do require training to be used safely and properly. For more information on dry suit selection, maintenance and use, you should consider taking the SSI *Dry Suit Diving* Specialty Course from your local SSI retailer.

Selection

When it comes time to select a dry suit, you will want to select the suit which best fits your diving (and financial) needs. Some of the factors you should take into consideration include: features, ease of use, ease of repair, guarantee, the manufacturer's reputation and history, and cost. A good dry suit can be a financial investment, but a quality suit will also last for many years if it is cared for properly.

Two different styles of dry suits.

■ **Fabric:** The materials used for dry suits will influence their performance and characteristics more than any other single factor. The five dry suit materials most commonly seen are closed cell neoprene, crushed neoprene, nylon, vulcanized rubber, and tri-butyl laminate.

■ **Features:** Different brands of dry suits come equipped with different features. Select the features most important to you. Some of the most common features to look for are attached boots, knee pads, attached hoods, and waterproof zippers. Other features include suspenders and ankle straps.

■ **Valves:** Dry suits have two types of valves: inflator and exhaust. Inflator valves input air into the suit to compensate for suit squeeze, and are normally located on the upper chest area. They require a low-pressure inflator hose to be added to your regulator. Exhaust valves remove air from the suit on ascent, and are located either on the left arm or upper chest. It is strongly recommended that your exhaust valve be variable, or adjustable.

■ **Size:** Since dry suits are designed for a somewhat loose fit, very few people need a custom suit. Most manufacturers build 4 or 5 sizes which probably fit about 90% of the population. Your SSI retailer will help you select the right size of suit.

Adjustment

When you purchase a dry suit, it is very important to adjust the neck seal for your individual neck size. If this is not done, the neck seal will be very uncomfortable. An authorized service person can help you adjust your seals if you have not received proper training.

Care and Maintenance

To rinse the outside of your dry suit, close the zipper and seal off the neck and wrist seals with rubber bands. Usually, there is no need to rinse the inside of your dry suit unless you perspired heavily, or if salt water leaked inside.

If your suit is equipped with latex neck and wrist seals, you should wash them with a mild soap to remove any body oils.

When drying your suit, hang it upside down so the water will drain out of, not into, your boots. If the inside of the suit is wet, turn it inside out and let it dry too.

The only acceptable lubricant for dry suit zippers is paraffin wax. Lubricate the zipper each time before you close the zipper.

Other tips on maintaining your dry suit can be found in the SSI *Dry Suit Diving Manual* or in your manufacturer's directions.

Field Repairs

There are various field repairs that can be done to combat minor problems with your dry suit. If you have a problem with your inflator valve sticking there may be some lint or dirt inside it. You may be able to pick out the lint, or clear it by flushing it with water. If the inflator valve still sticks, spray a small amount of silicone into the valve and then work it through the system by pushing the power inflator a few times. This may unstick the valve. Do not use silicone on exhaust valves.

A major tear to a seal will probably mean sitting the dive out. All of these repairs are best attempted after receiving instruction. Do not attempt any repairs that may affect dry suit performance, and do not dive if there is a problem with the valves or suit itself.

Storage

If your suit is a fabric material or vulcanized rubber, it should be rolled and stored in a bag. When rolling, make sure you cap the inflator valve, and roll so the valves are to the outside. If your suit is a closed cell neoprene, hang it over a bar or line at the waist so there is no strain on the zipper. Check your manufacturer's directions on how to store your model of suit.

All dry suits should be stored in a cool, dry, dark place. Avoid storage near electric motors or hot water heaters, because they produce ozone which can damage latex parts.

SUIT ACCESSORIES

Whether you are wearing a lycra, wet, or dry suit, accessories are available that offer additional protection from cold and abrasions. As was mentioned earlier, the biggest areas of heat loss are the head, neck, underarms and groin (Figure 1-14). By adding additional layers in these areas you can easily increase how warm you will be under water. Exposure suit accessories come in all thicknesses, depending on the amount of protection that is needed.

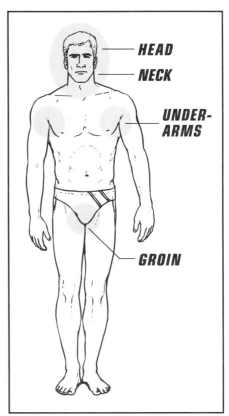

Figure 1-14   *The most critical areas of heat loss are the head, neck, underarms and groin.*

Hood

The hood can either come attached to the wet suit itself or to a vest, or it may come separate. For added warmth, the unattached hood should have a large skirt that can be neatly tucked under the wet suit jacket.

Boots

While dry suits will come with built-in boots, you will need some sort of foot protection with lycra or wet suits. There are many options available from lycra socks, to low-top tropic boots, to heavy duty neoprene boots. If you are planning on walking on rocks or boat decks, you may want a boot with a rubber sole for protection. Many boots also come with zippers for ease of donning. These boots work well in warmer waters, but allow water leakage that wouldn't be desirable in colder waters. The boot you select should match the thermal protection of your suit.

Gloves

Gloves should be selected much like boots, however, you may want to wear a glove that is lighter than your suit thickness if you need more flexibility in your hands. All thicknesses of gloves are available, from tropic reef gloves to dry gloves. Neoprene gloves are the most popular and they come in two styles: the five-fingered glove, or the three-fingered mitten. Some people prefer mitts in very cold water. Features to look for on gloves are zippers, velcro wrist straps, wrist seals, and textured palms for better gripping. All of these features are designed to make gloves more comfortable and practical in even the coldest water.

Gloves protect your hands from the cold, rocks, anchor chains and ladders, but realize that they do not give you the dexterity to handle delicate marine life that shouldn't be touched.

WEIGHT SYSTEMS

As we know, wet suits and dry suits increase your buoyancy and require the use of weights in order to get below the surface. For many years, the only option in weighting was the standard nylon belt with lead weights. Today, there are many types of weight systems that are more comfortable and aesthetic.

Selection

■ **Standard Belts:** While nylon belts are still the most common weighting system, the standard belt has been improved upon by offering options such as velcro shot pockets. These pockets simply velcro to the belt, stay in place, and make it easy to change the amount of weight you need.

Vinyl covered weights add color as well as protection. Vinyl weights also cause less damage to whatever they are dropped on.

■ **Pocket Belts:** Other weight options are the web or neoprene pocket belt. These systems offer pockets that you place the weights in and velcro shut (Figure 1-15). They provide flexibility in changing.

weight, as well as providing a little padding between you and the weights. Many divers feel these systems are more comfortable than standard belts.

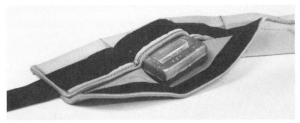

Figure 1-15   *Pocket belts can be more comfortable than the standard belt.*

■ Integrated Weights:

Another system that is available is weights that are integrated into your BC (Figure 1-16). Individual shot packs or weights are held into the BC by a velcro closure or a cable release system. By pulling a release mechanism, the weights drop from the belt, much like ditching your weight belt. The advantage of this system is that it is more comfortable because no belt is rubbing on your hips. Some people say this system also allows the diver to swim in a more natural, horizontal position. Another advantage is that the weights do not twist around your body so you always know exactly where the quick release mechanism is. The drawback is that your scuba unit becomes heavier with the additional weight.

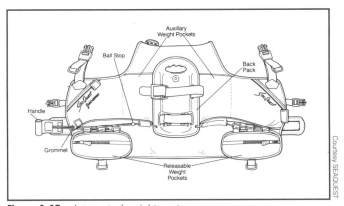

Figure 1-16   *Integrated weight system.*

Adjustment

Your nylon web or pocket belt may need to be adjusted to fit you better before diving. You should not have more than about six inches of extra belt when wearing your thickest suit and maximum amount of weight. Once you have decided on the length, trim the belt with scissors and then finish the cut by using a flame to melt the nylon fibers together (Figure 1-17). Now apply a light coat of wet suit cement to finish the edge and prevent fraying.

Another tip for nylon web belts is the use of weight keepers. These metal or plastic clips will keep the weights in place and prevent them from falling off the belt. This is handy if you are planning on using the same belt for a series of dives.

Figure 1-17 *Finishing the end of a nylon belt after trimming it to size.*

Care and Maintenance

Weights and belts are easy to care for, requiring only an occasional washing in fresh water. See your manufacturer's directions on how to care for your integrated weight system.

Field Repairs

It is advisable to carry an extra weight belt buckle in your spare parts kit in case yours breaks. You may also want to carry a lighter in case you need to fix any frayed edges.

Transportation

Most people do not travel with weights because of their added weight, however, it's a good idea to take your own belt. Depending on what type of integrated system you have, you may need to travel with your own shot packs.

Storage

When storing or traveling with nylon belts, roll them up to prevent heavy creasing. Hang or lay flat your neoprene belt to prevent creasing or damage to the neoprene from heavy objects.

The basic equipment for diving, the mask, fins, snorkel, exposure suit, and weight system, are generally easy to care for and should last for many years. While this equipment has no mechanical or electronic parts, it by no means says that they are less important.

Now let's move on to Chapter 2, where we will look at the scuba unit and the other equipment that is required for scuba diving.

CHAPTER 1
REVIEW

1. Divers who are serious will learn quickly that _____ their own equipment and knowing how to _____ for it will vastly enhance the diving experience.

2. The life of a silicone product is sometimes _____ to _____ times that of a black rubber product.

3. The nearsighted diver may choose to correct vision with optical lenses measured in _____.

4. A fin that is too stiff or has a very large blade may cause _____ or leg _____.

5. If you rarely use your snorkel, it is more important that you buy a _____ – _____ one.

6. Sunlight will _____ the fabric, _____ the nylon from the rubber, and will cause the neoprene suit to _____ over time.

7. Dry suits have two types of valves: _____
and _____.

8. The biggest areas of heat loss are the _____,
_____, underarms and groin. By adding additional _____ in these areas you can easily
increase how warm you will be under water.

9. Some people say that _____ weight
systems allow the diver to swim in a more
natural, horizontal position.

SCUBA
EQUIPMENT

2

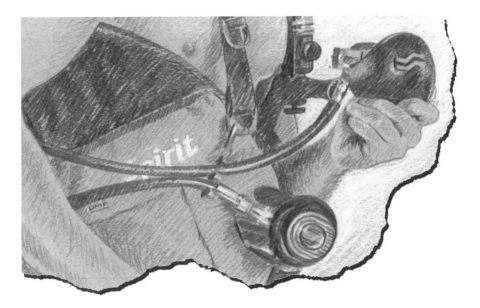

CHAPTER 2:
SCUBA
EQUIPMENT

The scuba unit is the diver's lifeline to the deep, and is the most critical equipment to keep in excellent condition. It is not only more complicated because of the mechanical and electronic parts, but also because your safety is so dependent on an operational scuba unit. A problem with one piece, the tank, the buoyancy compensator, the regulator or the instruments, could cause potential danger under water.

TANKS

Since the early days of diving, scuba cylinders have undergone an extensive evolution. The first tanks used for sport diving were actually war surplus tanks. They were wire-wound, which means that they had a small band of wire wrapped around them to contain the pieces should the tank explode.

While steel tanks were the standard throughout the 1950's and 1960's, in the 1970's aluminum tanks came on the market and started to gain popularity.

In today's market, one can find various sizes of tanks sold and used. For certain applications, one might even find double tanks being used, but these are primarily used by deep recreational divers with a lot of training and preplanning for their dives

Selection

No matter what size tank you purchase, the only materials still used to date for manufacturing are steel and aluminum. In order to have a better appreciation for scuba cylinders, let's take a look at how both aluminum and steel tanks are made, and examine how to read the tank markings.

■ **Aluminum Tanks:** Aluminum tanks are made of aluminum, magnesium, manganese, and silicone and are made through a process called cold-impact extrusion. Raw material is purchased by the manufacturer in long, round bars that are cut into smaller sections called billets. Each billet is stamped with an ID number so that it may be traced to its origins. Next, the billets are cleaned and etched in a chemical bath and coated with a special lubricant to make the extrusion process smoother and to eliminate surface defects. A ram pushes the billet into a chamber with the force of approximately 3500 tons. As the billet enters the press, it is at room temperature, but because of the tremendous force created, the shell that is produced comes out extremely hot. After extrusion, the shell is checked for defects and wall thicknesses. To create the neck, the end of the cylinder is trimmed and heated, and then pushed into a heading dye. Next, the valve threads are cut into the neck hole for the valve. To be sure that the tanks are uniform and evenly strong, they are heated to a very high temperature and cooled in a cold water cleaner, before they are heated again, at a somewhat lower temperature, and air-dried (called artificial aging). Tests are conducted on at least one tank out of each treated batch to make sure that they conform to required specifications. These tests include fatigue, to see what maximum pressure it can withstand. All tanks are hydrostatically tested to 5/3 their working pressure.

■ **Steel tanks:** To make steel tanks, large pieces of rolled steel are cut into small, easier-to-handle sheets that are annealed to 1300° F (704°C) for about 5 days. The steel is cooled slowly and punch-pressed into discs that are randomly sampled and tested, and then assigned a batch number. Each disc is pressed into the form of a tank without a neck, but much shorter, and is then drawn into a longer, narrower shape. Since this process affects the metal, it must be re-annealed, stripped of scale and then lubricated. Next, the tank is reheated to form the neck, and the valve threads are cut once the tank is cooled. Last, the tank is cleaned and then hydrostatically tested to 5/3 working pressure. After passing all inspections, the tanks are given serial numbers and stamped with the original hydro date. Most steel tanks have a galvanized exterior finish to prevent corrosion.

Steel tanks.

■ **Markings:** Scuba tanks must conform to government standards. Tanks without the correct markings are illegal, and reputable dive stores and air stations will not fill tanks which are not marked correctly (Figure 2-1). Tanks which do not meet prescribed standards should be condemned. If your tank is old, the markings may differ from today. Some of the older tanks might be stamped with ICC, Interstate Commerce

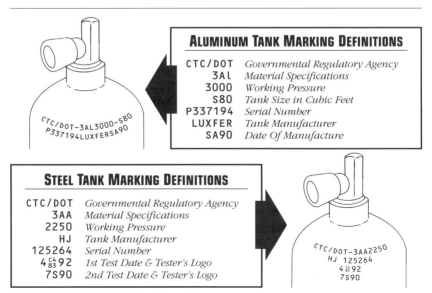

ALUMINUM TANK MARKING DEFINITIONS

CTC/DOT	*Governmental Regulatory Agency*
3AL	*Material Specifications*
3000	*Working Pressure*
S80	*Tank Size in Cubic Feet*
P337194	*Serial Number*
LUXFER	*Tank Manufacturer*
SA90	*Date Of Manufacture*

CTC/DOT-3AL3000-S80
P337194LUXFERSA90

STEEL TANK MARKING DEFINITIONS

CTC/DOT	*Governmental Regulatory Agency*
3AA	*Material Specifications*
2250	*Working Pressure*
HJ	*Tank Manufacturer*
125264	*Serial Number*
4$^C_{83}$92	*1st Test Date & Tester's Logo*
7S90	*2nd Test Date & Tester's Logo*

CTC/DOT-3AA2250
HJ 125264
4$^C_{83}$92
7S90

Figure 2-1 *Tank markings and meanings.*

Commission, which is the old version of DOT. Past markings for aluminum include SP6498 or E6498, while the new is 3AL. The previous marking for steel is 3A, which stands for carbon steel, while the new mark is 3AA. A few companies now offer a steel tank which has a working pressure of 3500 PSI and is made from a different alloy to increase its strength. This tank has a special marking of E9791.

■ **Accessories:** The few accessories for scuba tanks include tank protectors and tank boots. Materials used to make tank protectors range from a nylon mesh or cordura, to a lycra® sock (Figure 2-2). The tank boot and protector must be removed before a visual inspection.

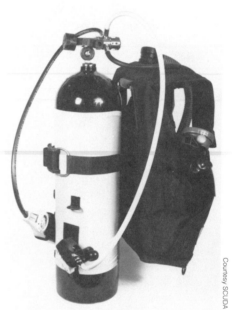

■ **Painting/Sanding:** When painting an aluminum tank, it is important to use a painting process which does not involve heat treatment. Heat changes the mechanical properties of the aluminum and can cause weaknesses. The same is true when attempting to remove the paint off an aluminum tank. Do not use

Figure 2-2 *Tank protector.*

Courtesy SCUDA

power sanders that can heat up the metal, or remove any of the metal surface. If any tank has been exposed to extreme heat, it should be hydrostatically tested and/or condemned.

Care & Maintenance

Proper maintenance, handling, and storage of diving cylinders is important due to the high pressure contents. When properly cared for, your tank will serve you for many years. This section is not intended to make you a qualified tank inspector, but it is intended to educate you on the types of damage to be aware of.

■ **Visual Inspections:** Visual inspection is required on a yearly basis by the diving industry . Most air stations require a current TIP®, or tank inspection, sticker before filling your tank (Figure 2-3).

Figure 2-3   *A current tank inspection sticker is required for filling tanks.*

Occasionally remove all exterior accessories (boot, stickers, etc) and check to see if your tank has any noticeable exterior damage. Damage to look for includes pitting, corrosion, cuts, gouges, dents and bulges. If you suspect damage be sure to take the tank to a qualified visual inspector for testing.

■ **Internal Corrosion:** Internal corrosion is one of the biggest concerns in tank maintenance. During a visual inspection, the inspector will look inside your tank for any traces of corrosion. Your tank may need to be tumbled or sand-blasted to remove the impurities. Moisture is the biggest cause of internal corrosion. To prevent water from entering your tank, have your tank filled at a reputable air station, and store tanks with some pressure (100-300 PSI), not allowing them to be drained completely of air.

■ **Hydrostatic Test:** The hydrostatic pressure test is performed at five-year intervals or whenever the inspector deems it necessary. The tank is filled with water in a sealed safety chamber and pumped to a pressure approximately ⅗ of the stamped working pressure of the tank. The test is required by the U.S. Department of Transportation. If the tank passes the test a new date is stamped on the neck of the tank. If not, the tank cannot be refilled.

Storage

Steel tanks should be stored with 100-300 pounds of air (7-20 bars) in them. A steel tank that is stored fully pressurizied may lead to accelerated oxidation or rusting, due to the high partial pressure of oxygen.

Aluminum tanks, however, should be stored fully pressurized. In the event of a fire, the heat would cause the burst disc to rupture before the tank would. When an aluminum tank is partially filled, the exposure to extreme heat might not cause the burst disc to blow, but it would cause the tank to lose tensile strength and explode the next time it is filled.

Transportation

As you can see, high pressure cylinders can cause a lot of damage if they are not properly handled. During transport, cylinders should be properly secured. A cylinder that is allowed to roll around can cause damage to itself, other equipment, or to people. Make sure that the valve is protected from damage. Last, never leave a standing tank unattended.

VALVES

The tank valve allows the air to flow from the tank to the first-stage of the regulator while providing a means for attaching the regulator to the tank.

Selection

Tank valves are made from brass or chrome-plated brass, which can cause a potential problem when used with an aluminum tank. Due to dissimilar metals and a reaction called electrolysis, or galvanic action, the valve can become frozen to the aluminum tank if not removed on a periodic basis. It is recommended that the valve be lubricated with a silicon lubricant when it is removed for the yearly tank inspection. If you are concerned, then you can

The three types of valves.

Courtesy SHERWOOD

have the valve lubricated more often. *Note: Steel tanks are not susceptible to this problem.*

Valves are manufactured with a valve snorkel or dip tube. This snorkel is screwed into the bottom of the valve and prevents any impurities inside the tank from entering the valve if the diver is in the head-down position. At one time, a plastic snorkel was introduced to reduce the problems of the dissimilar metals. There was one major drawback however. The snorkel was not made of a heat resistant thermoplastic and if the tank was in a fire, the snorkel would melt and seal off the valve, making the burst disc useless and impossible to bleed air from the tank. All manufacturers have returned to using metal snorkels.

There are basically three different types of valves on the market today that are divided into two categories—yoke and DIN connector. The yoke valve is the standard on most U.S. made tanks. The DIN connector is rated to be used at higher working pressures than the yoke valve and has been used extensively in Europe for many years. The DIN valve is now available to the U.S. sport diving market.

■ **"K" valve:** The "K" valve is a straight, 3/4" o-ring sealed yoke valve that was introduced to the diving industry in 1959. Since these were easier to use and the threads did not suffer the damage that older valves did, they quickly became the accepted standard in the industry, and are the standard today (Figure 2-4).

The "K" valve has a simple on/off mechanism that operates by pulling the seat away from the seat surface when the valve is on, so air flows from the tank. The "K" valve, or any other valve, should not be tightened too tight as it will cause damage to the seat.

Courtesy SCUBAPRO

Figure 2-4   *"K" Valve.*

■ **"J" valve:** In the days before the SPG, the "J" valve was very popular as divers had no way of knowing how much air they had until they simply ran out. A reserve was activated by a spring mechanism that restricted the air at a low tank pressure. The diver then moved the reserve lever to allow the remaining air in the tank to be used for the ascent.

The drawback to the "J" valve is that it was difficult to always have the lever in the right position. If the lever was not in the "up" position, there was no reserve, if it was not in the "down" position, you could not fill the tank. The "J" valve has continued to lose popularity and is rarely used or sold today.

■ **DIN Connector:** DIN stands for Deutsches Institute for Normung, which is the European agency that sets standards for gas equipment manufacturing, much like the Compressed Gas Association (CGA) in the U.S. DIN connectors are used on tanks that have a working pressure over 3000 psi.

DIN connectors come in various sizes, but the two standard for diving are the 200 and 300 bar connector. A bar equals 14.5 psi, a little less than 1 ATM (14.7 psi). Therefore, a 200 bar DIN connector is rated to 2900 psi, while a 300 bar DIN connector is rated to 4350 psi.

A DIN valve looks different than a regular valve because the regulator actually screws into it and the o-ring is captured under the connector. This eliminates the possibility of blowing an o-ring. The DIN connector operates on the same simple on/off principal as the "K" valve.

■ **Burst Discs:** A burst disc (or the over-relief valve) is a safety feature on all valves manufactured in the United States. In the event that the pressure in the tank becomes too high, the burst disc will rupture before the tank explodes. The discs are designed to rupture between tank rated pressure and the pressure that the tanks are subjected to during hydrostatic testing.

TABLE OF
CYLINDER PRESSURES vs. BURST DISC RANGES

Cylinder Working Pressure	Burst Disc Rupture Range (@160°F)
1800 psig	2700-3000 psig
2015 psig	3025-3360 psig
2250 psig	3397-3775 psig
2400 psig	3600-4000 psig
3000 psig	4500-5000 psig
3300 psig	4950-5900 psig
3500 psig	5250-5835 psig

Two old types of burst assemblies are the fusible plug and the unidirectional plug. The fusible plug had a lead filled center, and could blow out with a high velocity which was extremely dangerous. When the uni-directional plug ruptured, the air only escaped in one direction which caused the tank to spin uncontrollably.

Both of the older plugs need to be replaced with the newer burst disc assembly (Figure 2-5). The modern, multi-port design is safer, for if it ruptures, the air escapes in all directions. As tanks are refilled and emptied, the burst disc is continually under stress so it is recommended that it be replaced every 5 years. The entire burst disc assembly must be replaced as old and new parts must not be inter-changed. If the disc is not replaced periodically it may rupture under nor-mal conditions, which would be extremely danger-ous under water.

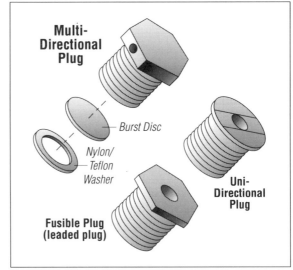

Figure 2-5 *Burst disc assemblies.*

Care and Maintenance

Both tanks and valves should be washed in fresh water after each dive. Salt and sand can corrode the valve opening if not cleaned properly. To avoid internal corrosion, vent the tank valve after each washing to prevent moisture and dust from entering the tank. Also vent the tank before filling it, so any moisture or dust in the valve will not be forced into the tank during the fill process.

BUOYANCY COMPENSATORS

One piece of equipment that has undergone major changes over the years is the buoyancy compensator, or "BC," as it is commonly called. Although designs have changed, the original intent is still the same: to provide positive surface flotation, to allow for neutral buoyancy at depth, and to aid in ascents.

The original BC was a front-mount,or horse collar, design that used a waist and crotch strap for securement. As you can imagine, this could be uncomfortable at times.

The next BC to hit the market was the back-mount style which became popular in the early 1970's (Figure 2-6). This style incorporated the tank into the flotation system which hooked over your shoulders and secured at your waist. While the back-mount BC is still popular, the original front-mount style is mainly used by snorkelers today.

The modern jacket style BC's that are popular today were introduced in 1977. This style integrated the tank into the BC, provided extra comfort, and allowed the diver to float comfortably in a vertical position on the surface with their head above the water (Figure 2-7). This style has evolved over the years, but jacket BC's are still the most popular today.

Selection

Fit is one of the most important parts of selection. The BC should be snug so it doesn't shift under water, yet it must be big enough to provide adequate lift on the surface. Many of today's jacket style BC's are designed for diving, not surface flotation. You must decide which feature is important to you. You will also need to select a BC that is designed for your intended use. For example, if you select a smaller, low-profile model that is designed to fit well, provide less drag, and pack easily for traveling, it will work perfect for warm water diving but will probably not fit over a heavy wet suit or dry suit (Figure 2-8). If your diving needs vary drastically, you may need to actually have two different BC's.

Courtesy STEVE BARSKY

Figure 2-6 *Back-mount BC.*

Courtesy SCUBAPRO

Figure 2-7 *Jacket syle BC.*

Courtesy SEAQUEST

Figure 2-8 *Low-profile BC designed for the warm water diver.*

■ **Single vs. Double Bladder:** The major difference between BC's is construction. Some BC's have an inner plastic bladder that is covered with a nylon shell which has the pockets, backpack and other features attached to it. This is called a *double bladder* BC. The majority of today's BCs, which are *single bladder*, are made by sealing two pieces of rubber-coated nylon together. The most common seam is heat sealed, and then tape is sewn on to finish the seam. This method is sturdy, yet inexpensive. A stronger seam is one that is radio frequency welded. This creates a stronger seam which is finished with tape and sewn. The strongest seam is one that has a piece of tape that is hand glued to the inside of the BC. The exterior of the seam is them finished by taping and sewing it. This process is labor-intensive which makes this type of BC more expensive.

■ **Integrated Weights:** Some manufacturers offer BC's that have integrated weight systems as was discussed earlier in this chapter under weight systems.

The various features that should be standard on all quality BC's were covered in the *Open Water Diver* course. These features include a low pressure inflator, an oral inflator, a dump valve, an overexpansion valve, and adjustment straps.

Adjustment

While a BC that is simply too big will be hard to adjust, one that fits well can be adjusted to increase comfort and performance. Your adjustment straps can be cut down so they fit over your thickest dive suit. Once they are sized right, trim the strap with scissors and then finish the edge as discussed in the weight belt section.

If your BC has a hard backpack, you can purchase a soft cover with a cummerbund from some companies to increase comfort. Other companies offer BCs with interchangeable pockets. This allows you to change the color of your BC to match different wet suits without having to buy a whole new jacket. Another way to personalize your BC is to add an alternate air source, or inflator-integrated regulator,

Figure 2-9 *Many hooks are available to attach equipment and accessories to your BC.*

in place of your power inflator. These regulators are discussed in the next section.

Hooks and clamps of all kinds can also be added to hold your octopus, console, game bags, and inflator hose (Figure 2-9). Be sure these clamps are quick-release should you need to have immediate access to any piece of equipment, such as your alternate air source, or should you need to ditch game bags or heavy items in an emergency situation.

Care and Maintenance

General BC care includes washing both the inside and outside of your BC thoroughly with fresh water after each use. Slosh water around inside your BC to make sure it cleans every corner. You may need to drain and refill it more than once to get rid of all the salt. Salt, sand and debris can corrode any mechanical part, so be sure to flush the dump valve and power inflator thoroughly. Your BC should also be dried completely to avoid internal molding.To dry your BC, fully inflate it and hang it upside down with the dump valve at the lowest point. As the water collects at the dump valve, it can be easily drained. Continue to let it dry until no more water can be drained out.

You should wash your BC occasionally with a mild cleanser that is also a conditioner and mold inhibitor. These cleaners are available from many various manufacturers through your local SSI retailer.

■ **Dump/Over-Pressure Valve:** Check your valve before each dive to make sure it over-pressurizes. If it is sticking open and allows air to vent, there could be dirt or debris inside the valve. You may be able to unstick it by flushing it with water. If the valve is stuck shut it will not release air, this may cause the valve to eventually rupture, causing damage to the BC. Do not dive if the valve is stuck open or shut. Take the BC to an authorized repair facility for service. To check your valve or bladder for leaks, completely fill the BC and submerge it in water. Bubbles will emerge from whereever the leak is occurring.

■ **CO₂ Cartridge:** Most manufacturers do not put CO_2 cartridges in BCs anymore because they are not necessary, but if your BC still has one you may want to have it removed. Your local dive store can help you update your BC.

If your BC still requires a cartridge, such as a snorkeling vest, be sure to occasionally remove it and lube the threads with silicone grease to prevent rusting, and to remove the cartridge during storage.

■ **Dump/Inflator Hose:** Sun, salt and age can wear a hole in the hose. To check for wear, stretch the hose and look between the corrugated seams. You will also want to make sure that it is attached securely to the BC and inflator, and that the cable ties are not damaged or missing. These cable ties can be easily replaced once your instructor shows you how. Occasionally lube the hose with silicone to keep it flexible. If the hose becomes damaged, it can be replaced by an authorized technician. If the dump valve is not working properly, the dump cord (inside the hose) may not be attached (Figure 2-10). Take it to your local retailer for servicing.

Figure 2-10 *The dump cord must be attached properly for the dump valve to work.*

Field Repairs

It is difficult to do any major repairs to your BC in the field beyond replacing cable ties or buckles. Because most manufacturers now offer a guarantee on their BCs, they do not recommend that you attempt to patch the bladder should it become torn or punctured. Any patch would only be temporary, and it may fail under water, jeopardizing your safety. Any BC with a damaged bladder should be taken back to the dive store so it can be repaired.

Storage

Buoyancy compensators should be stored only after they are clean and completely dry. Partially inflate your BC and hang it on a wide, plastic hanger. Store the BC in a cool, dry closet out of direct sunlight. Storing your BC in a wet, cold place such as a garage or outdoor shed may cause the over-expansion/dump valve to freeze shut. Be aware of this when using your BC on cold, winter days.

POWER INFLATORS

All BCs today are equipped to accommodate an inflator mechanism. If you have an older model, it should be retrofitted by your local retailer to accomodate a power inflator. The sport diving industry recommends that you do not dive without a low-pressure power inflator.

Selection

The two parts to the power inflator system are the inflator mechanism which is attached to the corrugated hose on your BC, and low-pressure inflator hose which is attached to your regulator first-stage. The quick-release connector on the inflator hose that attaches to the power inflator can vary in size between manufacturers. To insure that your inflator will operate properly, your low-pressure hose should come from the same manufacturer (be the same brand) as the inflator mechanism (Figure 2-11). The other end of the hose, which is threaded, is fairly standardized. This means that most any brand of hose can be attached to any regulator first-stage because they all fit the same size port.

While most power inflators operate the same, the buttons may be a different size, shape, or configuration. Some inflators may offer different features that make them easier to use. Your SSI retailer can help you select a power inflator.

Figure 2-11 *The power inflator and quick-release hose should be the same brand.*

Adjustment

The major adjustment you can make to the inflator is to change the mouthpiece. While some mouthpieces are permanently glued and are not meant to fit in your mouth, inflators that also function as a regulator must fit comfortably in your mouth. A new mouthpiece can easily be added to these types of inflators with a plastic cable tie. Your instructor or dealer can show you how to change a mouthpiece.

Care and Maintenance

The most important aspect of maintenance is to keep the inflator clean and corrosion free. Always soak the inflator in fresh water to remove any sand, salt and debris. To make sure the inflator/deflator is working properly, check it before every dive. Make sure it both inflates and deflates without sticking. If it sticks, soak it in warm water to remove any excess salt. If it still sticks, take it to a repair facility for servicing. To check the mechanism for leaks, put the inflator under water while the scuba unit is assembled. If any bubbles emerge from the inflator, there is a leak that must be repaired by a service technician.

Field Repairs

If the inflator/deflator mechanism is leaking or sticking in the field, do not dive. Never unhook the low-pressure inflator hose and dive with oral inflation capabilities only.

Transportation

When transporting your BC, make sure the power inflator mechanism is protected from damage. You may want to stick the inflator inside a wet suit boot or protective case. This is especially important if your inflator is also an alterate air source.

REGULATORS (ALTERNATE AIR SOURCES)

The evolution of diving equipment has produced many styles and models of equipment to satisfy the needs of today's recreational divers. However, the regulator has historically been comprised of only a few styles.

The single-stage, two-hose regulator was the first model to be used by divers (Figure 2-12). It was replaced by the two-stage, single-hose regulator which is still the model used today.

The early regulator contained one valve with a small orifice which produced greater breathing resistance with depth

Courtesy U.S. DIVERS / SKIN DIVER

Figure 2-12   *Early two-hose regulator.*

and low cylinder pressure, and because it had no purge valve in the mouthpiece it was more difficult to clear. With the design and production of the two-stage regulator in the 1950's, the single-stage regulator became rare by the early 1960's.

The two-stage regulator allowed the air pressure to be reduced twice: once in the first-stage and again in the second-stage. This allowed for smoother air flow and delivered air at a more constant pressure at depth, even with varying cylinder pressures.

The single-hose regulator, which became popular around 1965, had a purge valve at the mouth that allowed divers to clear the second-stage mouthpiece of water without having to remove it, plus the purge prevented water from entering the hose. Another factor that added to the popularity of the single-hose regulator was the ability to use a submersible pressure gauge, which very few double-hose regulators could accommodate. When the use of submersible pressure gauges became mandatory, the single-hose regulator became the clear choice of recreational divers.

By the late 1960's, many divers had taken it upon themselves to add an additional second-stage to their regulators which was to become known as an "octopus" regulator. The concept was to provide a back-up regulator in the event that the primary regulator malfunctioned. In 1979, the first inflator-integrated air source was introduced to the market. This sysem incorporated the power inflator and alternate air source into one unit. Today, similar systems are sold by many manufacturers.

The alternate air source (AAS) has taken on many different forms depending on the manufacturer, and is now a required piece of equipment for all divers certified by the sport diving industry. There are three styles of alternate air sources available: 1) a double second-stage, or "octopus", 2) an inflator-integrated air source, and 3) independent air source.

The style of alternate you select depends on your diving needs. Many people, especially deep divers, like having an octopus that is the same quality as their primary regulator, while other people like the convenience of an inflator-integrated system because it eliminates one regulator hose. Other divers like an independent system because it eliminates the need to share air from the same scuba unit. In fact, some people even carry an independent system in addition to an octopus or inflator system.

Selection

Detailed information on how regulators function can be found in the SSI *Open Water Diver* manual, Chapter Two, so function will not be covered in this manual. Instead, we will review what types of regulators are available for today's recreational diver.

Today's two-stage, single hose regulators are engineered and designed to provide you with a light-weight, safe, and easy-breathing piece of equipment. Choosing the regulator that is right for you is a function of performance, color, design, price and the manufacturer's warranty.

Whether you purchase a diaphragm or piston style regulator, you can be assured that today's regulators are the finest ever made (Figure 2-13). Consult with your local SSI retailer to find the regulator that is best for you.

Courtesy SHERWOOD

Figure 2-13 *Today's regulators are the finest ever made.*

Care and Maintenance

Regulators deliver your air, making scuba possible, and as such, require a higher degree of preventative care and maintenance than other equipment. Preventative maintenance is relatively easy and dictates that you have your regulator/AAS serviced by a trained technician at least once annually.

By thoroughly soaking the regulator with clean, fresh water after each dive, you will prevent corrosion of both the internal and external components of your regulator. Cleaning is particularly important when the regulator is used in salt water. When rinsing the regulator, make sure that the first-stage dust cap is in place, and do not press the second-stage purge valve when rinsing the mouthpiece This will decrease the chance of water entering the low pressure hose attached to the housing.

The Equipment Maintenance page in your Total DiveLog is an excellent tool for keeping track of regulator maintenance and warranty information.

> ***NOTE:*** *Never attempt to disassemble the first-stage or second-stage regulator, or replace any o-rings or parts. This should only be done by a trained technician. Any tampering with the regulator will most likely void your warranty.*

■ **O-Ring Leaks:** Each hose that attaches to the first-stage will have a "static" o-ring that must be replaced if it malfunctions (Figure 2-14). If you detect a leak in the first-stage, the o-ring is probably damaged. Your authorized dealer will be able to replace the o-ring for you.

Figure 2-14 *Each hose that attaches to the first-stage will have a "static" o-ring.*

■ **Free Flowing:** On occasion, your second-stage may free-flow due to sand or dirt that is lodged between the diaphragm and second-stage housing. You should first attempt to flush away the debris with water, and by tapping the housing on your hand. If this does not work do not use the regulator, and take it to an authorized dealer for servicing.

■ **Leaking Second-Stage:** The second-stage exhaust tee covers the exhaust diaphragm. The diaphragm will allow water to enter the second-stage if it is cracked or not seated properly. An authorized technician will be able to reseat or replace the diaphragm.

Another item typically overlooked is the second-stage mouthpiece. Small holes in the mouthpiece will cause water to leak into your mouth as it becomes worn. To replace the mouthpiece, remove the old one by cutting the cable tie, placing the the new one on the housing, and re-securing it with a new plastic cable tie (Figure 2-15). You can also change mouthpieces if yours is uncomfortable or if it doesn't fit your mouth prop-erly. Replacement mouth-pieces can be purchased at your local SSI dive store.

Figure 2-15 *Use a plastic cable tie to secure a new mouthpiece.*

Remember, always be careful when making any repairs to your regulator. You may cause the regulator to malfunction and may void your warantee. Always seek the help of a trained technician when your regulator begins to breathe poorly, or when there is a leak in the hose, the first-stage, or the second-stage.

Storage

How you choose to store your regulator can also be considered preventative maintenance. Be sure that the regulator is completely dry, and then coil the hoses loosely (in a circular pattern) into a protective regulator bag. Hanging the regulator by the hoses will put undue stress on them, decreasing their life.

Ozone and sunlight are two of the most destructive forces working on rubber products. To protect your rubber hoses, be sure to store your regulator in a dark, cool place and away from electric heaters which produce ozone as a by-product.

INSTRUMENTS

As human beings, we are blessed with five senses that provide continuous information about the world in which we live. Because we live on the land, our senses are well-adapted to the familiar air atmosphere, but not the foreign liquid environment below the water. In this strange, dense environment, other creatures possess highly-adapted senses. Fortunately, we are intelligent enough to invent instruments that overcome our shortcomings.

Our instruments allow us to determine how deep we are, how long we have stayed, in which direction we are traveling and, perhaps most important of all, how much precious air we have left. With instruments, we gain information that restores a high degree of safety, comfort and fun to diving.

CONSOLES

In the mid sixties, when instruments were becoming popular, divers strapped depth gauges, compasses and watches to their wrists, creating clumsy instrument panels on their arms.

Then came the instrument console. By organizing your instruments into one panel, it provides all the information you need in one convenient place. This frees your arms up, makes dressing faster, and makes forgetting a gauge impossible. Most gauges today are purchased in a ready-made console, but some people still purchase individual instruments to customize a console that fits their needs.

Selection

Most instruments can be either *analog* (mechanical) or *digital* (electronic) (Figure 2-16). Electronic gauges are generally more accurate and require less maintenance than analog gauges, plus they usually integrate many functions into one small unit. While electronic units can be more expensive, analog consoles allow you to add instruments as your budget allows, starting with a depth and pressure gauge, and adding a compass, timing device, or computer later. Almost every manufacturer designs a console for its instruments, but not all brands of instruments fit into all consoles. Some consoles can also hold other accessories, such as knives and slates for further convenience.

Courtesy DACOR

Figure 2-16 *A console with both analog and digital instruments.*

Adjustment

There are very few changes you can make to your instruments to improve them. Faceplate protectors can be added to prevent scratches, or a strap or clip to attach the gauge to your BC is an excellent idea. This prevents equipment drag by making swimming easier, while it protects the environment by preventing gauges from banging on reefs.

Care and Maintenance

Instruments are easy to care for and maintain. After diving, wash them in fresh water to remove dirt and salt. Occasionally, remove the instruments from the console and soak them in fresh water. Batteries should be replaced according to the manufacturer's suggested maintenance schedule or when low-battery indicators warn of problems.

Transportation

Most instruments are susceptible to minor damage during travel. Damage can be prevented with a padded gauge bag, or by placing both the regulator and console in a padded regulator bag.

Courtesy/ U.S. DIVERS

Instruments are available in a variety of styles; either grouped in consoles or sold individually.

Storage

By storing your gauges properly you can prolong their life, and well-maintained instruments should last practically forever.

Make sure the gauge is clean and salt-free before storing, even behind the console or the protective rubber housing. After the gauge is completely dry, store it in a padded bag for protection.

Now that we have looked at consoles, let us look at each instrument individually at see how care and selection may vary.

SUBMERSIBLE PRESSURE GAUGE

In the early years, divers had no instruments so they relied on nerve and faith that they would have enough air to complete a dive. When the pressure gauge was finally developed in the mid-sixties, divers could tell at a glance what their exact air supply was. Ultimately, the Submersible Pressure Gauge, or SPG, became one of the most significant improvements in diving equipment and diver safety.

Selection

The SPG is connected to the high pressure port of the regulator's first-stage, which allows it to access the quantity of compressed air before the first-stage converts it to intermediate pressure.

To determine the actual tank pressure (in psi or bars), most standard analog SPG's use a *bourdon tube*, which is a flattened tube that is spirally wound inside the gauge housing behind the face plate. When compressed air is forced into the tube, it tends to straighten or unwind the tube. As air is consumed, the tube relaxes or winds back up, which moves the indicator needle on the gauge back toward zero.

Features to look for in an SPG include a scratch resistant face, a swivel head, and a luminous faceplate. The SPG should be able to indicate pressure beyond the maximum pressure of your tank. Because many tanks now hold in excess of 3500 PSI (238 bars), your SPG should read pressures in excess of 4000 PSI (288 bars).

Care and Maintenance

To prevent water from flooding the gauge, make sure you replace the regulator dust cap after each use and before washing.

At least once a year you should take your gauge in for servicing to test its accuracy. At this time, the major o-rings, which are located at the regulator high pressure port and the gauge swivel head connection, should also be inspected. If the o-rings look flat, cracked, or imperfect in any way, they should be replaced. If the o-rings look fine, they should be lubricated. The burst plug should also be cleaned and inspected annually by a service technician. The burst plug requires servicing to insure its function and reliability.

You should also ocasionally inspect the hose for bulges, cracks and tears. A weakness in the hose could cause it to rupture. The weakest spot is where the metal connectors attach to the hose. Hose protectors made of flexible plastic or stiff rubber prolong the life of the hose by preventing the metal connector from pinching the rubber.

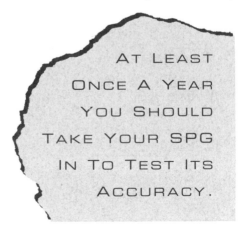

AT LEAST ONCE A YEAR YOU SHOULD TAKE YOUR SPG IN TO TEST ITS ACCURACY.

Field Repairs

Unless you have an extensive spare parts kit, including an extra high pressure hose and o-ring, there is little you can do in the field for a problem SPG. If your SPG is leaking it can probably be fixed if you have the proper o-ring and silicon grease. *Do not replace an o-ring with one that is "close enough."* If the escaping air only causes a tiny trickle of bubbles, it may be safe for diving, but fix it as soon as you get home. If the bubble stream is strong, do not dive with the gauge. Any tear or bulge in the hose requires replacing the hose before diving again.

DEPTH GAUGE

Depth gauges, along with dive watches, were the first instruments widely used by scuba divers because the importance of monitoring depth and bottom time became clear early on.

Selection

The two most popular analog gauges, and most accurate at depth, are the *oil filled gauge* which uses a bourdon tube, and the *air filled gauge* which is activated by a diaphragm. These gauges are sealed mechanical devices that react to pressure, which cause a needle to move. Older styles of depth gauges such as the open bourdon tube are no longer common.

The *capillary gauge* is the most accurate depth gauge in shallow water up to 30 feet (9 metres) (Figure 2-17). It is a plastic air-filled tube with one end open to the water. It works on the principle of Boyle's Law. As you descend, the air inside the tube compresses, to one-half volume at 33 feet (10 metres), to one-third at 66 feet (20 metres), and so on. This is why the shallow depths are so far apart on the faceplate, while the deeper depths are close together, and why capillary gauges are considered accurate at shallow depths, but not deep.

Some analog depth gauges include a maximum depth indicator

Figure 2-17 *Capillary depth gauge.*

Figure 2-18 *Depth gauge with a maximum depth indicator needle.*

to tell you the deepest depth reached during the dive (Figure 2-18). While these indicator needles are convenient for dive planning, the excess friction caused by this needle can slightly decrease the accuracy of the gauge, but at an acceptable tolerence level.

Electronic, or digital depth gauges are also popular and commonly come as part of an integrated, electronic console. Unlike analog gauges, electronic gauges require batteries that must be replaced.

Care and Maintenance

While digital gauges require new batteries, analog gauges require a periodic recalibration, which should be done by the manufacturer to ensure the gauge's accuracy. Keep your gauge working correctly by following the manufacturer's suggested service schedule.

TIMING DEVICE

The original timing device was a diving watch, which was considered the serious diver's status symbol, a tradition that still holds true to some extent. Timing devices now come in many more varieties than watches, such as dive timers, dive computers and other integrated instruments.

Selection

A timing device's main function is to help you monitor bottom time so you stay within your dive plan. A dive watch with a rotating bezel or stop-watch works well, however, with a bezel you can pre-set the time you need to surface. Look for bezels that click into place, or only move clockwise because there is less chance of it slipping and losing your reference point.

Dive timers are simply pressure-activated stopwatches. They are designed to turn on as soon as you begin your descent, and turn off after surfacing. There is less chance for error because you do not have to manually turn it on or off. This makes dive timers handy devices.

Care and Maintenance

While some batteries in timing devices are consumer replaceable, others must be serviced at the factory so they remain properly sealed against pressure. Your local dive store or jeweler may not have the proper equipment to perform this job or to test the result. Check the directions on your device for how to replace batteries so as not to void your warranty.

COMPASS

Compasses are considered essential equipment by experienced divers, but they require additional training and practice to be used to full advantage. In fact, an entire SSI *Navigation Course* is available, which includes extensive information on selecting, maintaining and using compasses. Only a brief overview of compasses is covered in this manual.

COMPASSES
ARE CONSIDERED
ESSENTIAL
EQUIPMENT BY
EXPERIENCED
DIVERS.

Selection

There are a variety of compass styles available, including top-reading, side-reading and watch band. Compasses are available in wrist band styles, or mounted in a console, or on a slate. The most versatile compass is one that is both top-reading and side-reading, because it can easily be used in a variety of circumstances. Important features to look for in a compass include, a magnetic needle, 360° markings, a liquid-filled housing, and a lubber line. Other features are a movable bezel, luminescent markings, an index mark, and a reciprocal course mark.

DIVE COMPUTER

The first widely used dive computer became popular in the early sixties, but not until the early eighties did a model similar to the current digital dive computers become available.

Today's computers all use a theoretical model to calculate a hypothesis of how your body absorbs and eliminates nitrogen, so the computer acts as a simulation of what your body is actually doing. Therefore, caution should be exercised when using a dive computer because a theoretical model can only approximate the average human physiology, and your individual physiology could differ from the model. Therefore, training in dive computer theory and proper use is strongly recommended. For this reason, SSI offers a specialty course in *Computer Diving.*

Selection

There are a number of excellent dive computers on the market today, offering many powerful features. All dive computers monitor depth and time while computing your theoretical nitrogen absorption (Figure 2-19). Most also maintain a log of your dives in memory, which includes the dive number, maximum depth and total bottom time.

Computers also time your surface interval and calculate repetitive dive profiles at various depths for subsequent dive planning. In addition, most computers monitor your ascent rate to ensure you ascend between 30 and 40 feet-per-minute. Should you accidentally stay longer than the suggested bottom time, some computers have a decompression mode for your safety.

Other features to look for include the ability to adjust to higher altitudes for use above sea level, and the ability to monitor tank pressure so air consumption can be computed. While these are the most common functions, more are available, and new developments are forthcoming every year.

A tiny computer chip allows these small instruments to offer these powerful functions. Like other high technology products, dive computers are changing rapidly, becoming smaller, more powerful and less expensive. Computer technology is the area where the major advances in diving equipment are occurring, setting the path for future breakthroughs in safety and training.

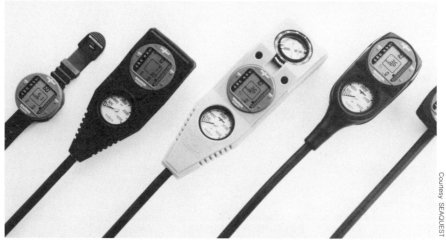

Courtesy SEAQUEST

Figure 2-19 *Dive computers monitor depth and time while computing your theoretical nitrogen absorption.*

Care and Maintenance

Batteries are the primary concern with dive computer maintenance. Some use batteries that must be changed at the factory, while others require batteries that can be store bought, but can be difficult to find in some remote diving locales. Make sure the batteries are changed according to the manufacturer's maintenance schedule to avoid problems. Most dive computers have a low-battery indicator which provides sufficient warning to avoid problems.

Any computer problems must be handled by a professional dive store or the manufacturer. Keep your computer clean and well protected when traveling.

Now that we have looked at all of the basic equipment needed for scuba diving, we will go on to Chapter 3 and look at the specialized equipment and accessories that can add safety, comfort and enjoyment to the sport.

CHAPTER 2
REVIEW

1. Tanks without the correct markings are illegal, and reputable dive stores and air stations will not _____ tanks which are not _____ correctly.

2. The hydrostatic pressure test is performed at ____ year intervals or whenever the inspector deems necessary.

3. There are basically three different types of valves on the market today that are divided into two categories: _____ and _____ connector.

4. General BC care includes washing both the _____ and _____ thoroughly with fresh water after each use.

5. To insure that your inflator will operate properly, your low pressure hose should come from the same manufacturer as the _____ _____.

6. The two-stage regulator allowed the air pressure to be reduced _____: once in the first-stage and again in the second-stage.

7. _____ gauges are generally more accurate and require less maintenance than analog gauges.

8. Because many tanks now hold in excess of 3500 PSI (238 bars), your submersible pressure gauge should read pressure in excess of _____.

9. The most popular analog gauges, and the most accurate at depth, are the oil filled which uses a _____ _____ , and the air filled gauge which is activated by a _____.

10. Today's dive computers all use a theoretical model to calculate a hypothesis of how your body absorbs and eliminates _____.

SPECIALIZED EQUIPMENT

3

CHAPTER 3:
SPECIALIZED EQUIPMENT

Some pieces of equipment such as flashlights and knives are considered accessories, even though they are useful on every dive. Other items such as propulsion vehicles, metal detectors, and sonar devices are fun, and enhance your hobbies. Many advanced divers enjoy using accessories as a way to increase their safety and interest in diving.

ACCESSORIES

Depending on what type of specialized diving you are doing, such as night diving, many diving accessories may be considered essentials. Knives, lights, communication equipment and flags all have a specific purpose, and add to the safety of the sport.

KNIVES

The divers knife is an important tool under water. It can be used for cutting, prying, or communication by tapping on your tank. Although most knives are constructed of stainless steel, proper maintenance is essential to keep them in good shape.

Adjustment

The dive knife is most commonly worn on the diver's lower leg, however, you may want to consider attaching it to other equipment such as your BC so you don't have to worry about putting it on before each dive. To attach it to a front-adjustable BC, simply remove the straps from the sheath and use plastic cable ties to hook it to your BC shoulder strap (Figure 3-1).

Care and Maintenance

Rinse your knife in fresh water after every dive and allow it to dry thoroughly. Spray your knife with a light coat of silicone to help seal it. If possible, occasionally dismantle your knife to clean and lube each part.

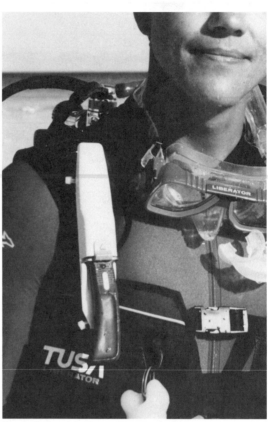

Figure 3-1 *A knife can be attached to a BC with plastic cable ties.*

Should your knife begin to rust, rub it out with Naval Jelly or any non-rusting abrasive, and then reapply silicone to protect it. When your knife becomes dull, sharpen it with a sharpening stone that is made for knives.

You should also replace your rubber sheath, straps and retaining ring as they begin to wear out. This will help prevent the loss of your knife when diving.

LIGHTS

There are two basic styles of underwater lights: rechargeable and non-rechargeable (Figure 3-2). Non-rechargeables are usually less expensive but you must continually replace the batteries. Rechargeable units may take up to 15 hours to recharge, limiting the number of times it can be used within a short time span. If you are traveling out of the country, find out what electrical current is used so you will know if you will be able to recharge your lights. Lights come in a variety of models from large primary lights, to smaller flashlights. Chemical lights, strobe lights, and accessory lights are also available. Information on selecting, using, and maintaining lights, is available in the SSI *Night/ Limited Visibility Diving* course.

Figure 3-2 *Rechargeable light.*

Care and Maintenance

All underwater lights are sealed with one or more o-rings. These o-rings must be kept clean and well lubricated to insure the water tight integrity of the light. Lubricate the o-rings with a light coat of silicone grease periodically. Be sure to also clean the sealing grooves of the light. *Remember to always safely dispose of used batteries!*

Field Repairs

If you should accidentally flood your underwater light, you should rinse all parts with fresh water and dry them as quickly as possible. Test the light to see if it still functions properly. If it does not, return it to the manufacturer for repairs.

If your light beam is dim, or non-existent, even when the light

Figure 3-3 *Gently buff the contact points to remove any corrosion.*

has fresh batteries in it, you may have a problem with the electrical connection. Gently buff the contact points with steel wool, sandpaper, or even a pencil eraser to remove any corrosion that could be interfering with the electrical flow (Figure 3-3).

Storage

Before storing your light, make sure the o-rings are clean and free of any sand or debris. This debris may make it difficult to open the light after a year in storage. Also, to avoid internal corrosion and damage, do not store batteries inside the light. Read your manufacturer's directions for specifics on storing your light, especially if it is a rechargeable model. To increase the life of both rechargeable and non-rechargeable batteries, store them in a cool place, such as the refrigerator (not the freezer).

COMMUNICATION

As you know, it can be very difficult to communicate under water, especially in an emergency. Manufacturers are constantly trying to develop new products to make communication easier.

Underwater Communication Devices

Because sound travels four times as fast under water, even dull noises can be heard easily. This is why tapping your tank with a knife or other object works well. In an emergency situation, mechanical devises that emit a loud noise are effective. For one-on-one conversation, hand signals and slates are still the only means of communication until some type of speaking devise is developed for recreational divers. Speaking devices are already available in full-face masks for commercial divers.

Surface Communication Devices

When a diver is on the surface in high wind or waves, it can be very difficult to get someone's attention, especially if you have drifted quite a ways away from the boat. A whistle that is attached to your BC is one basic device to use, mechanical alarm systems are also very effective. Other communication devices include signal lights and smoke flares, but these are not as widely used. One last device is more of a means of signaling than communication, but it works well in high seas and is easy to carry in your BC pocket (Figure 3-4). It is a florescent

Figure 3-4 *Surface signaling device.*

colored nylon tube that can be inflated with your regulator second-stage. When inflated, it stands approximately 6 feet (1.8 metres) in the air. This device is sold under many names, from a variety of manufacturers.

ASCENT MONITOR

Another, easy-to-use accessory is an ascent monitor (Figure 3-5). It easily hooks to your console hose or wrist and it lets you know how fast you are ascending. This simple device replaces the need to study your watch and depth gauge on ascent, and is handy for people who do not have a computer with an ascent function.

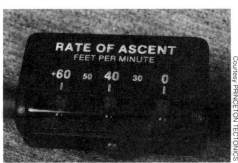

Courtesy PRINCETON TECTONICS

Figure 3-5 *Ascent monitor.*

FLAGS AND FLOATS

It's hard for boaters to see divers on the surface, and it would be impossible for boaters to know when divers are under them if not for a system of communicating these facts. The diver's flag serves this purpose. The two kinds of flags used are the *recreational diver's flag* and the *alpha flag*, or the international "diver down" flag. The recreational diver's flag is red with a diagonal white stripe. It says, "There are divers below; keep clear, and travel at a slow speed." It is flown only when divers are actually in the water. The recreational diver's flag is governed by tradition, and in some places by law.

The alpha flag is blue and white with a "V" cut into one side (Figure 3-6a). It is flown from boats and says, "This vessel has divers below and maneuverability is restricted." It is most often used during commercial dives when divers are tethered to the boat by hoses or lines. The alpha flag is flown only in international and inland navigable waterways.

Flags should be displayed on some sort of float, unless they are attached to the flagpole on a boat (Figure 3-6b). This could be a buoy, lifesaver, inner tube,

Figure 3-6a *Alpha flag.*

surfboard, or small raft. Larger rafts and boats make good floats in deep water situations or on repetitive dives, because you can store equipment in them or use them in emergencies.

Figure 3-6b *Recreational diver flag.*

DIVE LOG

The dive log is not really an accessory any more, it is a necessity. In fact, many resorts and dive stores require a log for proof of certification and diving experience. The SSI *Total DiveLog* is more than a log book for recording dives, it is also a valuable tool for charting your diving future. The DiveLog provides credit for logged dives through recognition stickers at the completion of each level. The DiveLog also shows you how to continue your training and move onto more advanced levels such as Specialty Diver, Advanced Open Water Diver, Master Diver, and the prestigious Century Diver.

The Dive Log is not really an accessory any more — it is a necessity.

BAGS & BOXES

A variety of sizes and styles of equipment bags have been developed to help store and protect almost every piece of scuba equipment. With the investment you make in your equipment, and the time that is put into customizing it, it is worth a little extra time and money to store it properly and lengthen its life.

EQUIPMENT BAGS

By now you realize the importance of equipment maintenance, and proper protection plays a key role. Your equipment bag should be big enough to hold all diving equipment except the tank and weights. It should be made of durable material and have heavy duty zippers, handles and seams. Shoulder straps and backpack styles are useful when traveling or walking to your dive site.

Some bags have separate compartments for wet and dry gear, so you can pack your clothes with your equipment, while others are designed to just hold snorkeling gear. There is a bag designed for almost every need and every size load.

In addition to your storage/traveling bag, a mesh bag is useful on boats and on trips to warm climates where your gear is constantly wet. The mesh fabric allows the equipment to breathe and prevents mold growth. These bags easily roll up for traveling.

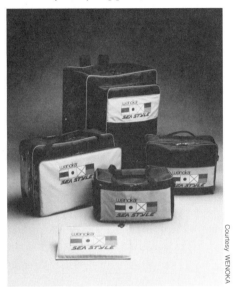

Courtesy WENOKA

Various equipment bags.

ACCESSORY BAGS

There are also a variety of small bags that can be used to protect your gauges and accessories. Regulator bags will keep your regulator and console clean and safe, while instrument bags will add an extra layer of protection. Most instrument bags zip around the console leaving the hose out. Regulator bags will usually also hold small, breakable items such as lights and computers, and can be used as carry-on bags for traveling.

STORAGE BOXES

Storage boxes are also available for sensitive equipment such as masks, computers and cameras to prevent breakage. Some boxes are simple plastic boxes, while others are crush-proof and o-ring sealed for airtight, watertight protection. These boxes also work well for first aid, or spare parts and repair kits.

EQUIPMENT FOR SPECIAL ACTIVITIES

As scuba divers continue to gain experience and log dives, many begin to get interested in specialty activities that further increase diving excitement. Underwater photography, hunting, and treasure collecting are just a few hobbies available to the diver. All of these activities require specialized equipment that can be very complex. Care, maintenance, and field repairs are best covered by the manufacturer's information and warranty. Your local SSI dive store will also be able to assist you in selecting and caring for any specialized equipment.

CAMERAS

Photography is one of the favorite pastimes for divers. While still photography remains the favorite, videography is gaining wide-spread popularity with the invention of camcorders. While video cameras require a housing for use under water, still cameras can either use a housing or be self-contained. A self-contained camera is o-ring sealed itself, and may have a built-in flash, or the capability of attaching a strobe the camera body. These cameras are by far the most popular with recreational divers.

The most important aspect of camera or video care is to keep the internal camera mechanisms dry. This means the seals must be kept in perfect shape at all times. Your SSI retailer or manufacturer can assist you with camera maintenance.

DIVER PROPULSION VEHICLES (DPV'S)

Scooters, or underwater propulsion vehicles, can be a fun, easy way to travel a considerable distance while minimizing air consumption (Figure 3-8). DPV's have rechargeable batteries, and accessories, such as lights or gauges, that can be attached to the scooter body.

Be aware when using a DPV, for it is very easy to get too deep too fast, to ascend too quickly, and to get too far from the boat or shore. You do not want to travel farther and longer than the battery will take you, or you may have to drag your DPV back to the boat!

Figure 3-8 *Diver using propulsion vehicle.*

METAL DETECTORS

Metal detectors can be very fun, and profitable, for treasure collectors. Coins, jewelry, gold, and other lost valuables can be recovered while diving. Remember, every state has different laws governing treasure hunting. It would be advisable to know them. In fact, some countries forbid the use of metal detectors and a diver can suffer a severe penalty just for bringing them into the country. You should call a local dive shop, the consulate, or the tourism bureau before planning on bringing a metal detector into a foreign country.

The three major classes of detectors are transmitter–receiver, very low frequency, and pulse induction. Each type is ideally suited to a different environment and type of target. Your local SSI retailer will be able to help you learn more about underwater metal detectors (Figure 3-9).

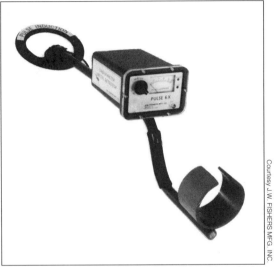

Courtesy J.W. FISHERS MFG. INC.

Figure 3-9   *Your local SSI retailer will be able to help you learn more about underwater metal detectors.*

LIFT BAGS

Should you find a large item, or should you just need to bring up a recovered anchor or weight belt, you may need a lift bag to assist you. Lift bags are tied to the object and then inflated using a separate air system and tank. Special instruction is required to safely use lift bags. Ask your SSI retailer about a Specialty Course in *Search and Recovery*.

HUNTING EQUIPMENT

Many divers, especially on the coastal U.S., enjoy hunting and collecting game such as fish and lobster. There are various tools available for hunting such as spearguns, pole spears, abalone irons, game collection bags, slurp guns and nets.

Be aware of hunting laws and seasons before collecting or taking any game. Your local retailer will be aware of game laws and may offer a Specialty Course in *Spearfishing*.

KAYAKS

Kayaks have been popular for years with river runners and life guards, but in recent years have taken off in the diving industry. A diving kayak is designed to carry a diver and his or her gear away from beaches and over-dived reefs. They are specially designed to hold dive gear and a flag. You can anchor the boat at the site, or tow it along with you. More information is available from kayak manufacturers or your local SSI store. It is recommended that you receive training in using a kayak before diving with one.

SONAR

Sonar devices are another accessory for diving. Although they do not create their own fun, they are a valuable tool for finding it. Sonar devices can send and receive high frequency pulses to help you locate the nearest object, whether it is a wreck, the dive boat, or a lost buddy (Figure 3-10). More information on sonar can be found at your local SSI retail store.

Courtesy SCUBAPRO

Figure 3-10   *Sonar device.*

SPARE PARTS AND REPAIR KIT

As we have mentioned throughout this manual, minor field repairs may be necessary for equipment from time to time. A spare parts kit may allow divers to continue a dive that otherwise would have to be cancelled. A recommended list of spare parts is listed in the appendix of this manual. In addition to these listed items, you may want to carry extra equipment such as a mask, snorkel, gloves and light. These may come in handy if yours is irreparable.

These items can be neatly assembled into a dry storage box to create a kit, or you can even purchase pre-packaged kits from many manufacturers. If your kit is pre-packaged, make sure it includes all of the items you will need in the appropriate sizes.

A handy diving tool is also available that replaces the need for a selection of wrenches and screw drivers (Figure 3-11). This repair tool is designed to fit the standard sizes of screws, plugs, and fasteners used on scuba equipment.

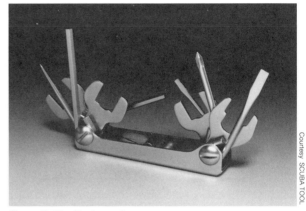

Courtesy SCUBA TOOL

Figure 3-11 *Scuba tool.*

Accessories can add fun and excitement to your dive; in addition, they can also increase your safety and comfort on specialty dives such as night dives. Now let's move on to Chapter 4 and look at how to travel with equipment.

CHAPTER 3
REVIEW

1. Some pieces of equipment such as flashlights and _____ are considered accessories, even though they are useful on every dive.

2. If your light beam is dim or non-existent, even when the light has fresh batteries in it, you may have a problem with the _____ _____.

3. Hand signals and _____ are still the only means of communication until some type of _____ device is developed for recreational divers.

4. In addition to your storage/traveling bag, a _____ bag is useful on boats and on trips to warm climates where your gear is constantly wet.

5. Underwater _____, hunting and _____ collecting are just a few hobbies available to the diver.

6. A _____ _____ kit may allow divers to continue a dive that otherwise would have to be cancelled.

TRAVELING WITH EQUIPMENT

4

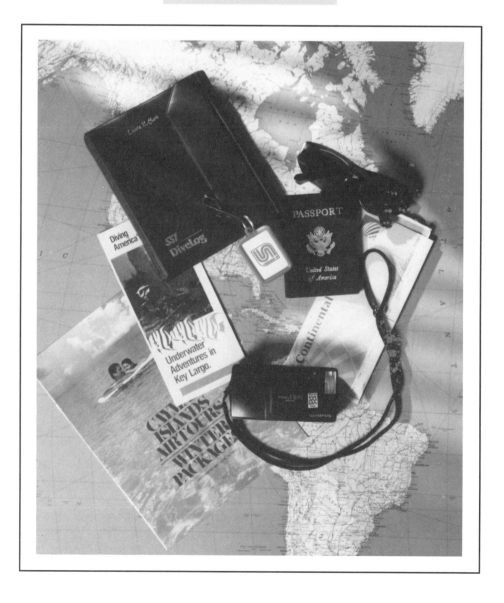

CHAPTER 4:
TRAVELING WITH EQUIPMENT

Traveling with scuba equipment requires some special planning and considerations to help ensure a successful diving vacation. Of course, the farther away you travel, and the more isolated it is once you get there, will have a big bearing on your level of preparation. However, no matter where you are traveling to, all dive trips require the same basic steps of preparation that are covered in this chapter.

TRIP PREPARATION

Before leaving for your trip, confirm that you have all of the necessary equipment. Some of your equipment may need to go to your local dive store for servicing, while other pieces may need to be sent back to the manufacturer for repairs. You may even want to purchase a special piece of equipment, or something you wished you would have had on your last trip (Figure 4-1). Allow plenty of time — at least one month — to get your equipment in top shape.

Figure 4-1   *You may want to purchase a special piece of equipment for your trip.*

Purchasing New Equipment

If you are diving in a different locale than normal, or will be doing different types of diving such as night diving, you may need to purchase some new equipment. A warm-water wet suit may make you more comfortable, while a new computer will help you get more logged dives in. Evaluate your equipment needs.

Pre-Trip Maintenance

If a piece of equipment was giving you trouble on the last trip, have it serviced. If you have not used your equipment since last season, get it serviced before diving with it. The more time you spend now preparing for the trip, the less time you will have to waste at your destination.

If you keep an up-to-date record of your equipment maintenance in your log book you will know how long it has been since a certain piece, such as your alternate air source, has been in for servicing (Figure 4-2). Your log book can help you keep track of warranty information also.

After your equipment has been serviced, you may want to try it out in the pool to make sure it functions and is adjusted properly. It is better to find problems now than after you have jumped in the water for your first dive.

Figure 4-2   *Keep track of equipment maintenance in your divelog.*

Marking Equipment

Once your equipment is ready to go, be sure and mark it so it can be easily identified at the dive site, and to protect it against loss or theft (Figure 4-3). After all, there may be more than one pair of fins like yours on the boat or at the beach.

Your wet suit, BC, and plastic items can all be marked with a permanent marker or with rubberized marking paint. You will probably want to mark your suit, BC and other items inside the neck, or in a semi-hidden spot. Metal items, such as your regulator, can be engraved. A good temporary marking system is to use the same color of electrical tape on every item.

Figure 4-3 *Mark equipment before packing.*

Check your marking system before every trip to make sure your name is still legible, and that all serial numbers, makes, and models are recorded in your dive- log equipment record. This will provide a record should any piece of equipment be lost or stolen on your trip.

■ **Customs:** If you are traveling out of the country you should register your equipment, especially photo and video gear, or any expensive, foreign-made items, with the customs office. This will prevent having to pay duty when returning from your trip. Most major cities and all international airports have a customs office that can register your equipment.

■ **Insurance:** Before traveling, check with your renter's or home owner's insurance to see if equipment loss, damage or theft is covered under your policy. If it is not, you may want to take out a temporary insurance policy from your insurance agent, travel agent or airline carrier. Do not count on an airline to automatically cover lost luggage to the full value of the equipment, especially if it is photo gear. You may also want to check your health and accident insurance to make sure you are covered in case of a diving accident. If you are not, you may want to purchase supplemental insurance from a carrier such as the Divers Alert Network (DAN).

Packing For The Trip

No matter where you are traveling to, packing light is a big concern. Even car trips may be a big squeeze if you are carrying diving and camping gear. The major difference with airline travel is baggage handling. You control your luggage on a boat or in a car, but not on an airplane. Also, airlines have strict limitations on baggage weight, size, contents and quantity.

When taking your equipment on a plane, make sure your gauges and other sensitive equipment are protected. Pack your regulator in a padded bag and tuck it in the middle of your equipment, or put your gauges and second-stage into your wet suit boots, gloves and hood for protection. Some people will even choose to put their regulators, computers, or cameras in their carry-on luggage. Cameras and camera accessories should be packed in a foam-lined, crush-proof suitcase.

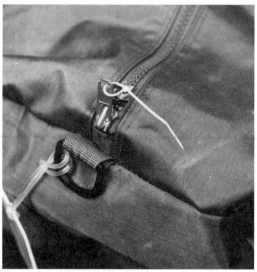

A good way to prevent your baggage from opening enroute is to secure the zippers with plastic cable ties (Figure 4-4). Remember to bring along something, such as nail clippers, to snip open the zippers for the customs agent, and to bring extra ties to resecure the bag.

Figure 4-4 *Plastic cable ties will prevent zippers from opening enroute.*

■ **Baggage Limits:** Baggage regulations vary from airline to airline, but it is safe to say that they get stricter as you travel farther from the U.S., and as the aircrafts get smaller. Most U.S. airlines allow 2 checked bags and 2 carry-on bags. Any excess baggage costs extra. Foreign airlines usually allow less, and they may charge you for any excess weight also. Be sure to find out what baggage limits you will have to follow. Your travel agent or airline should be able to help you.

Avoiding Lost Luggage

Lost luggage can be a nightmare, and is a sure way to ruin a vacation. Dive gear can not only get lost, but it can also be a target for theft.

■ **Disguise Your Bags:** Although dive bags are great organizers that have been designed to carry dive gear, they can tip off theives that you are traveling with valuable equipment. You may want to select a dive bag with little or no diving insignia, or you may want to pack in a standard suitcase and transfer your equipment to your gear bag at the dive site. Hard sided suitcases provide better security and protection, plus they usually lock.

■ **Mark Your Bags:** Make sure that you mark your bags with a heavy duty luggage tag on the outside, plus mark your suitcase on the inside in case your luggage tag gets torn off (Figure 4-5). This will allow you to identify and prove the bag is yours, or track it down if it is lost.

Figure 4-5 *Mark your bags both inside and out to prevent lost luggage.*

When you check your bags at the airport go to the airline counter, not the curb, plus, double-check your destination tags the airline attaches to make sure the bags are routed properly. Last, be prepared to be able to describe your bags should you need to file a lost luggage report. Know the size, color, brand, style, and any distinguishing features, in addition to the contents.

DURING THE TRIP

During the dive trip, keep your equipment organized in your gear bag before,during and after every dive. This will help avoid lost or damaged equipment. You will want to wash your equipment in fresh water after every dive and store it in a secure area at night. Some dive stores and liveaboard boats will provide lockers on site, or you may want to take your equipment back to your room or car.

Record Tips In Dive Log

Throughout your trip, write down any equipment that you wished you owned, anything that needs to be fixed or adjusted, or any tips that you might have picked up from other divers. This could include ideas

WRITE DOWN EQUIPMENT YOU WISH YOU HAD, ANYTHING NEEDING REPAIR, OR TIPS YOU PICKED UP FROM OTHER DIVERS.

from how to attach your octopus regulator, to what brand of dive light they recommend. Other divers are a great source of information, and dive trips are a great time for sharing ideas.

Repacking

You should wash and thoroughly dry your equipment before packing it. You may want to soak your equipment in fresh water after your last dive and allow plenty of time for it to dry. Wet dive gear can become smelly, moldy, rusted and corroded on the return trip. When packing, take as much care to protect your equipment on the trip home or it may get damaged.

AFTER THE TRIP

Unfortunately, your equipment maintenance is not over as soon as you get home. By properly caring for your equipment now, you can make the next trip less work up front.

Soak Equipment Overnight

Whether you've been at the local lake for the weekend, or somewhere far away, soak your equipment overnight in the tub once you get home to loosen any excess salt and debris. Salt can cause rust and corrosion if it is not removed. Allow your equipment to dry thoroughly before storage.

Post-trip Maintenance

Take care of any repairs, broken straps, and other problems now while you still remember. This is where your list from your trip comes in handy. Make sure you have lubricated and maintained everything as was discussed earlier in this manual.

You may also want to make any purchases or adjustments to equipment that you noted on your list. If the equipment you want is not affordable right now, start saving for it or put it on lay-away. By taking care of any problems or purchases now, you will be ready to go the next time someone invites you on a weekend or an exotic get-away.

Scuba diving is an equipment intensive sport. Your comfort, safety, and enjoyment under water depends on the condition of your equipment. With proper maintenance, your equipment will last for many years. As you learn to adjust, maintain, and customize your equipment it truly becomes your diving "partner", especially tuned to your own body, to help increase your comfort and safety under water.

CHAPTER 4
REVIEW

1. Traveling with scuba equipment requires some special _____ and considerations to help ensure a successful diving vacation.

2. If you keep an up-to-date record on your equipment maintenance in your _____ _____ you will know how long it has been since a piece of equipment has been in for servicing.

3. If you are traveling out of the country you should register your equipment, especially _____ and _____ gear, with the customs office.

4. Make sure that you mark your bags with a heavy duty luggage tag on the outside, plus mark the _____ in case your luggage tags gets torn off.

5. Unfortunately, your _____ _____ is not over as soon as you get home. By properly caring for your equipment now, you can make the next trip less work up front.

APPENDIX

1
Equipment Checklist

2
Spare Parts & Repair Kit

3
Equipment Record

4
Maintenance Record

5
*How SSI's
Total DiveLog System
Works*

APPENDIX 1

Equipment Checklist

- [ ] Mask
- [ ] Snorkel & Keeper
- [ ] Fins
- [ ] Diving Suit
- [ ] Boots
- [ ] Gloves
- [ ] Hood
- [ ] Weight Belt
- [ ] Weights
- [ ] Buoyancy Compensator
- [ ] Backpack
- [ ] Tank(s) Full
- [ ] Regulator
- [ ] Alternate Air Source
- [ ] Pressure Gauge
- [ ] Watch or Timer
- [ ] Depth Gauge
- [ ] Compass
- [ ] Knife
- [ ] Whistle
- [ ] Decompression Computer
- [ ] Thermometer
- [ ] Defogging Solution
- [ ] Dive Light/Batteries
- [ ] Chemical Light

- [ ] Dive Flag
- [ ] Dive Tables
- [ ] Log Book
- [ ] Certification Card
- [ ] Speargun
- [ ] Extra Points
- [ ] Goody Bag
- [ ] Fishing License
- [ ] U/W Camera
- [ ] Flash or Strobe
- [ ] Batteries
- [ ] Film
- [ ] Slate
- [ ] Spare Parts Kit
- [ ] Swim Suit
- [ ] Towels
- [ ] Suntan Lotion/Sunscreen
- [ ] First Aid Kit
- [ ] Money for Emergency Calls
- [ ] Money for Air Fills
- [ ] Money for Galley & Tips
- [ ] Passport
- [ ] _____
- [ ] _____
- [ ] _____

APPENDIX 2

Spare Parts & Repair Kit

☐ Fin Straps & Buckles

☐ Mask Straps & Buckles

☐ Snorkel Keeper

☐ Knife Retaining Kit

☐ Knife Leg Strap

☐ Needle and Thread

☐ CO_2 Cartridges

☐ O-rings, Bulb for Light

☐ Batteries

☐ Dust Cap

☐ Regulator Port Plug

☐ Regulator Mouthpiece and Cable Ties

☐ O-rings

☐ Silicone Spray

☐ Silicone Grease

☐ Wet Suit Cement

☐ BC Patch Kit

☐ Buckles for BC

☐ Buckle for Weight Belt

☐ Screwdriver (Straight & Phillips)

☐ Pliers

☐ Crescent Wrench

☐ $\frac{5}{32}$-Inch Allen Wrench

☐ WD-40 ®

☐ _____

☐ _____

☐ _____

☐ _____

☐ _____

APPENDIX 3

Equipment Record

ITEM	COLOR	MANUFACTURER	MODEL OR SERIAL NO.	DATE OF PURCHASE	PURCHASED FROM
MASK					
SNORKEL					
FINS					
WET SUIT					
REGULATOR					
A.A.S.*					
PRESSURE GAUGE					
BUOYANCY UNIT					
BACK PACK					
WATCH					
DEPTH GAUGE					
COMPASS					
TANK					
LIGHT					

*A.A.S. = Alternate Air Source

APPENDIX 4

Maintenance Record

BY	DATE	BY	DATE	BY	DATE	BY	DATE		

APPENDIX 5

H ow SSI's Total DiveLog System Works...

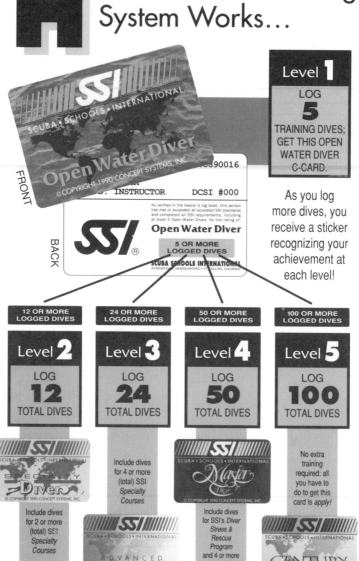

FRONT

BACK

As verified in the bearer's log book, this person has met or exceeded all accepted SSI standards and completed all SSI requirements, including at least 5 Open Water Dives, for the rating of:

Open Water Diver

5 OR MORE LOGGED DIVES

SCUBA SCHOOLS INTERNATIONAL
INTERNATIONAL HEADQUARTERS • FT. COLLINS, COLORADO

Level 1

LOG **5** TRAINING DIVES; GET THIS OPEN WATER DIVER C-CARD.

As you log more dives, you receive a sticker recognizing your achievement at each level!

12 OR MORE LOGGED DIVES

24 OR MORE LOGGED DIVES

50 OR MORE LOGGED DIVES

100 OR MORE LOGGED DIVES

Level 2
LOG **12** TOTAL DIVES

Level 3
LOG **24** TOTAL DIVES

Level 4
LOG **50** TOTAL DIVES

Level 5
LOG **100** TOTAL DIVES

Include dives for 2 or more (total) SSI Specialty Courses

Include dives for 4 or more (total) SSI Specialty Courses

Include dives for SSI's Diver Stress & Rescue Program and 4 or more (total) SSI Specialty Courses

No extra training required; all you have to do to get this card is apply!